Northern Plains Public Library

3 3455 02397 8403

SUPER BRONCOS

FROM ELWAY TO TEBOW TO MANNING

D1025803

BY WOODY PAIGE AND MIKE KLIS
FOREWORD BY JIM NANTZ

NORTHERN PLAINS
PUBLIC LIBRARY
Ault, Colorado

Vigliano Books

© Paige/Klis, 2014
Published by Vigliano Books

Cover Design: Marija Vilotijevic
Cover Photograph © Evan Semón

All rights reserved. No part of this publication may be reproduced, stored in or introduced into a retrieval system, or transmitted, in any form, or by any means (electronic, mechanical, photocopying, recording or otherwise) without the prior written permission of the copyright owners. Any person who does any unauthorized act in relation to this publication may be liable to criminal prosecution and civil claims for damages.

*To Broncos fans everywhere who have
enjoyed and endured the wild ride.*
– Woody Paige

*To my younger brother Bryan, who has always been there for
me, his wife Tina, and their wonderful children, Rachel and
Jordan. Sometimes, kids, uncle Mike fails to remember, but
he never forgets.*
– Mike Klis

Table of Contents

SUPER BRONCOS

FROM ELWAY TO TEBOW TO MANNING

FOREWORD

That magic of a six-game winning streak is back in a big way. Denver is going on to New England. The Broncos have just won it on the first play of overtime.

– Jan. 8, 2012 –

We're going to see an attempt here at an all-time record field goal in NFL history. We believe it'll be from 64 yards for Matt Prater. Sixty-three is the record, of course. And, now, for the all-time mark from 64. Matt Prater's kick is . . . good! History is made!

– Dec. 8, 2013 –

Hello, friends.

When Tim Tebow and Demaryius Thomas connected on that 80-yard touchdown pass play, and Matt Prater kicked that 64-yard field goal, those were just two of the many magical moments for the Denver Broncos.

Over the past quarter century, I was fortunate enough to bear witness to the Broncos making history during many incredible games while I was doing the call for CBS Sports.

I've had the pleasure to cover three of the most remarkable quarterbacks who've played the game: John Elway, Peyton Manning and, yes, Tim Tebow.

I was at Mile High Stadium for John Elway's final home game on Jan. 19, 1999, when he led the Broncos over the New York Jets for

i

the AFC Championship and he did a victory lap. I was at Sports Authority Field on Jan. 8, 2012, for Tim Tebow's last home game with the Broncos, which was his most meaningful and memorable – the overtime victory against the Pittsburgh Steelers and the aftermath celebration with 75,970 cheering fans. And I was at the stadium once more on Jan. 19, 2014, when Peyton Manning and Tom Brady would meet for the AFC Championship. Manning passed for exactly 400 yards and two touchdowns, outdueled Brady, and the Broncos advanced to the franchise's seventh Super Bowl.

See what I mean?

The past three seasons, particularly, have been special and often spectacular for the Broncos. My CBS partner, Phil Simms (the MVP Super Bowl quarterback in a New York Giants' victory against, I hesitate to say, the Broncos and Elway) and I were in Denver often. In fact, I think we called more Broncos games during those three seasons than any other national network team.

There was a lot of great action for Phil and me to talk about in those 20 games. There will be a lot of great reading for you in *The Super Broncos – From Elway To Tebow To Manning*, co-authored by Woody Paige and Mike Klis.

Allow me to interrupt and tell you about how I first came to know my old... long-time friend Woody.

In 1984, two years after graduating from the University of Houston, I was working in Salt Lake City, doing local telecasts of the Utah Jazz games with the legendary Hot Rod Hundley. The Jazz's first playoff series since moving from New Orleans (thus the name) was against the Denver Nuggets. The Jazz lost Game 3 to trail 2-1 in the best-of-five. The next day Woody wrote in his column in *The Denver Post* that the Jazz "have no heart" and couldn't possibly win the series. Well, that accusation struck deep at the heart of the Jazz, and, with the score tied at 124 late in the fourth quarter of Game 4 in Denver, Utah rookie Thurl Bailey hit a long jumper. The Jazz won. At the final game back in Salt Lake City, everybody in the arena wore "heart" stickers, and the song *You Gotta Have Heart* blared over the sound system.

The Jazz won the game by 16, and coach Frank Layden and the players publicly, and sarcastically, thanked Woody for the motivation. Nuggets coach Doug Moe blamed Woody for the loss. Woody went on to appear daily on ESPN's popular *Around The Horn* and I went on to join CBS Sports. We see each other regularly at The Masters, the Final Four, NFL games, and the Super Bowl and I always remind him of the Jazz-Nuggets series.

As a sidebar, Woody and I and a few others shared dinner and wine in 2000 at a restaurant near Pebble Beach (site of the U.S. Open that week) with Jean van de Velde, the pro-golfer from France who, the year before, experienced one of the most infamous meltdowns in the history of the major tournaments during the British Open at Carnoustie. He squandered a three-stroke lead on the final hole when he made a triple-bogey seven, and lost in a playoff.

Van de Velde was a delightful dinner guest with his 'c'est la vie' attitude. I never found out if Paige said "that's life" after the Jazz beat the Nuggets. I had spent the evening with two of the biggest losers in sports history: van de Velde and Paige.

Just kidding.

This past NFL season, after Peyton and Eli Manning played against each other in New Jersey and the Broncos won easily, my wife Courtney and I were having dinner with my agent (who also represents Peyton) at our hotel near Newark Airport when Woody suddenly appeared. He had finished his column and returned to the hotel. Even though it was the second game of the season, we talked about the real possibility of the Broncos returning to MetLife Stadium for the Super Bowl.

It happened. I was as surprised as anyone that Peyton and the Broncos lost the Super Bowl after that sensational season, especially after the job John Elway had done putting that team together and bringing Peyton to Denver. I've known both Peyton and John forever it seems.

1998 was Elway's last season, and the 1st year CBS got NFL broadcasts back. I was hosting *NFL Today* and was on site the day John played his last game at Mile High. After the game I went up on the podium and gave the AFC Championship Lamar Hunt Trophy to Pat Bowlen. I interviewed Pat, Mike Shanahan, and then Elway. Denver would go on to Miami to beat Atlanta giving John his second Super Bowl win and back-to-back MVP titles.

I remember holding a microphone as John was basically saying goodbye to Denver and his home base and I remember the stadium shaking. It was a poignant moment in Broncos history. John went for a run around the field. It was special for me to be there. None of us knew John would be back in a different role. He was a leader then on the field, and *the* leader now off the field.

On Jan. 28, 2012, I had a front row seat when Tim Tebow defied all logic. I've done the call for some surreal sports events: Tiger winning at the Masters, UConn becoming champions at the Final Four, the night the lights went out in New Orleans, but I'll never forget the Broncos-Steelers playoff game.

The whole thing was bizarre. Nobody's ever had such a run like Tebow, except maybe for quarterback-kicker George Blanda back in the old AFL. I'm old enough to remember that year when Blanda found a way to win all the games at the end for about a six-week stretch. Tebow put together a breath-taking streak, and the mother of all was winning that playoff game against Pittsburgh, Super Bowl champs the previous year.

I'll give you a story. This was the first time the NFL brought in the new overtime rules for the playoffs. I had always been a big opponent of the old overtime system in which a team could get the kickoff and win with a field goal. I liked the new rule. If the team that got first possession in overtime didn't score a touchdown, the other team would get a chance.

On the eve of that game, just to cover my bases, I talked to Broncos coach John Fox about what he would do if there was an overtime. Would he choose to defend if he won the coin toss? Would he want the ball? He said he would choose to receive. Then we went to Boulder, where the Steelers were staying, and I asked Pittsburgh coach Mike Tomlin the same question.

Tomlin foreshadowed what happened the next day. He didn't know it, but he wrote the entire script. He told me that there's no way he would kick the football if he won the toss because he didn't want an 80-yard miracle touchdown play by Tebow to win it. He said, "You know, the way things happen with Tebow, you don't want any kind of freakish thing. So, with these new rules, I'm not going to lose without having the football."

I said to him, "Coach, they didn't score a touchdown last week against Kansas City. How're they going to score on the first play of overtime? You know they're not going down and scoring a touchdown on your defense. You know you're going to get a touchback on the kickoff. You put Tebow on the 20."

And he said, "I'm not going to give him the football."

So, of course, the next day, the way the game unfolded, it was overtime. The way it worked out, Denver won the coin toss and got the ball, and the very first play of overtime, there was an 80-yard strike from Tebow to Demaryius Thomas for the touchdown. Game over. It was exactly what Tomlin had said in Boulder.

We put a graphic up on TV explaining how the new rules worked, but people still didn't know. I can't tell you how many people told me that when Thomas took off for the end zone, they didn't think the game was over. They thought Pittsburgh would get a chance to respond. Thomas didn't even realize the game was over. He didn't totally understand the rule. Before you could absorb the new rules, the play was there right in front of you.

I talked to Broncos offensive coordinator Adam Gase and Chargers coach Mike McCoy this past year about that play. McCoy, of course, was the offensive coordinator then and Gase was the quarterback coach. McCoy called that play from the sidelines. They had been sitting on that play all game long. Before the overtime started McCoy got over to the sideline with Tebow and Demaryius Thomas and told them about the play and that it should be open.

Gase told me this year that as he watched the defense set up for the opening play, he saw cornerback Ike Taylor inching up, getting close to the line of scrimmage. Gase started screaming into the headset to McCoy: "This is going to be it. It's going to be wide open. We could break this one for a big one."

He was so animated describing what happened. He knew McCoy made the right call and Pittsburgh was unwittingly playing right into the Broncos' hands. The play was perfect. Taylor was virtually at the line of scrimmage when the play started. Tebow throws it as Demaryius, who lined up on the left side, breaks across the field. The pass is right there. Thomas makes the catch and there's nobody to stop it. I remember making the call that Thomas had the ball, then was at mid-field, stiff-armed the last man and was at the 40, 30 and, like that, in the end zone.

It was such an amazing play, Gase and McCoy are still talking about it two years later. I'm sure Tomlin is still thinking about it two years later as well. And we're all still talking about how the first-ever overtime game with the new rules ended on the opening OT play.

For a short time, the Broncos had three of the biggest headliners in football history. But when the deal was struck for Peyton, Tebow had come to an end in Denver. It had to happen. I go way back with

Peyton, to his college days at Tennessee. Those are the dark days of CBS when it comes to the NFL. The network had lost the rights to FOX. We got them back four years later, and had the AFC instead of the NFC, so that's why I called so many of Peyton's games with the Colts and the Broncos.

And there I was, back in Denver for Brady and New England vs. Manning and Denver in the AFC Championship for maybe the last time (who knows?). I know how important that one was for Manning and the Broncos after the defeat to Baltimore the previous year. So much was hinging on that game against Tom after the Patriots' 24-point comeback in New England during the season. I thought that was perhaps, outside the Super Bowl, the most significant victory in Peyton's career.

The Broncos and I have been alive for almost the same number of years. I was born in 1959, the same year the AFL was being formed with eight cities, including Denver. I don't remember their first season, but I remember seeing many of the rest of their seasons. So have Mike Klis and Woody Paige.

Mike, one of the NFL's best beat writers with *The Denver Post*, and Woody, a brilliant writer, have written thousands of stories and columns about the Broncos over a combined 40 seasons of covering the franchise. They've given us the definitive account of the 2013 season when the Broncos were the wildest west offensive show in NFL history. Woody and Mike have provided us with a complete historic perspective of the Broncos: the good and the bad, the best and the brightest.

This foreword is the beginning, and I look forward to doing the call on many more memorable moments for the Broncos.

– Jim Nantz, March 14, 2014 –

Overture:
WOODY PAIGE

*Don't let it be forgot that once there was a spot, for one
brief shining moment, that was known as Camelot.*

– King Arthur –

March 20, 2012 was the day the Earth stood still for the Denver
Broncos.

For one brief shining moment, the NFL franchise had three of the
most renowned quarterbacks in league history in its employ.

Elway was the Broncos' executive vice president of football operations. Tebow was on the Broncos' roster as the returning starting
quarterback. And Manning had chosen to sign with the Broncos as
the team's new starting quarterback.

When worlds collide . . .

Past and present of the Broncos, meet the immediate future.

"I know what kind of player Tim Tebow is and what kind of person that he is," Manning said during an afternoon press conference.
"What an awesome year he had… and if Tim Tebow is here next
year, I'm going to be the best teammate I can be to him, and he and I

are going to help this team win games. If other opportunities present themselves for him, I'm going to wish him the best. He's going to be a great player wherever he is."

Several minutes later in a hallway, when Manning and I were alone, he said: "Go, Big Orange."

It was not a reference to the orange jersey hanging over his suit coat shoulder. Manning cheerily was offering up the long-time popular chant referring to the athletic teams at the University of Tennessee, Manning's alma mater, and mine. Manning would be back in orange for the first time since he graduated from UT. I said in reply: "Well, you finally beat Florida."

Manning laughed. He knew what I was talking about. During his four seasons at Tennessee, Manning didn't beat the Gators or win a national championship. Tebow had been on two national championship teams at Florida.

Less than 24 hours later, Tebow would be traded from the Broncos by Elway. The Volunteer had beat the Gator.

Never before, though, had three celebrated (and in some quarters despised) quarterbacks been with the same organization at the same time, no matter how briefly. Two had produced incredible seasons with the Broncos. The third would produce his own.

Sure, the San Francisco 49ers once had Joe Montana and Steve Young on the same team, and both eventually would be inducted into the Hall of Fame. Bart Starr, Brett Favre, and Aaron Rogers have played quarterback for the Green Bay Packers, and all three someday will be in the Hall of Fame together. The Dallas Cowboys had Roger Staubach and, later, Troy Aikman; the Steelers had Super Bowl-winning quarterbacks in Terry Bradshaw and Ben Rothlisberger, and Sammy Baugh ended his Hall of Fame career in Pittsburgh. Bob Griese and Dan Marino played with the Miami Dolphins, Johnny Unitas and Manning with the Colts, and, now, Andrew Luck. So there will be debates about the franchise with the best collection of quarterbacks. But the Broncos are in the lead paragraph because of the legend and the notoriety of Elway, Tebow, and Manning (and don't forget Jay Cutler literally passing through).

Super Broncos: From Elway to Tebow to Manning, aptly and distinctly describes the Broncos: their glorious and inglorious history, and their Super Bowl victories (two) and losses (five), including the latest.

And, in particular, this is a book about their quarterbacks.

As Richard Burton, starring as the mythical King Arthur on Broadway in *Camelot,* implored the boy he had just knighted:

"Don't let it be forgot…"

Overture:

MIKE KLIS

All of New Jersey anxiously awaited the Broncos' arrival at Super Bowl XLVIII.

At least the mayor of Jersey City was eager.

The Broncos' team plane landed at the Newark airport on Sunday, Jan. 26, a week before their Big Game with the Seattle Seahawks. The players, coaches, executives and essential personnel climbed aboard the buses and whooped it up during their police-escorted drive.

They pulled up to a well-wishing mob that had gathered in front of their team hotel. The bus stopped and Broncos' football operations boss John Elway climbed off.

He was immediately approached by a handsome young man wearing a blue overcoat, who somehow managed to fight his way through fans, media, security, and state troopers.

"Mr. Elway," the man said, "would you sign this for me?"

Patrick Smyth, the Broncos' media relations director, quickly took control of the situation.

"Sir," Smyth said, "he has to keep moving. He has to meet the mayor of Jersey City."

The young man smiled.

"I am the mayor of the Jersey City," said Steven Fulop, who had been on the town's city council since he was 28 and is now 36. "I have here a welcoming proclamation on behalf of Jersey City."

Should have heard Elway cackle. He signed the proclamation, posed with Mayor Fulop for a photo, and the Broncos' team that Elway assembled had officially arrived at Super Bowl XLVIII.

A small group of flight attendants from Norway had just checked in but before they went to their rooms, they leaned over the third-floor railing to see what the fuss was about.

"The Broncos are a team, right?" one said, serious as the hotel's $15 Jersey grilled cheese sandwich.

Amid the frenzy, some perspective.

Most of the players seemed to be wearing new suits.

"There's a lot of guys wearing different colors I never thought I would see them wear," said Broncos special teams captain David Bruton.

Wes Welker sat before a media throng wearing a salmon-colored coat. That was salmon, right?

Not 15 minutes after arriving, Broncos coach John Fox walked up the short plank to a cruise ship parked along the back of the Hyatt hotel on the Hudson River where the Broncos' press conferences would be held. I was standing right at the entrance to the boat as he came aboard (I probably should have been handing out leis).

"Oh no," Fox said upon realizing the first person he saw in New Jersey was an old face from Denver. "Don't they have security around this place?"

The Broncos arrived in New Jersey loose and in good spirits. After all these years, there was something right about Champ Bailey having his own Super Bowl press table. He had played in 12 Pro Bowls, more than any cornerback in NFL history. This would be his first Super Bowl.

His thoughts on Day 1?

"This is probably the worst part right here," Bailey said. "Sitting here answering these questions that I'm going to have to answer all week."

Sorry, Champ. The mid-week interview sessions would be the highlight. It would get so much worse.

"You've got to be kidding me!" a mic'd-up Bailey said from the sidelines as Percy Harvin returned the second-half kickoff for a game-clinching touchdown.

It was no joke, Champ. Harvin's return put the Broncos down, 29-0.

Whereas, the Broncos, champions of the AFC, were doomed from the first snap.

Whereas, Steven Fulop, the handsome, young mayor of Jersey City, was nowhere to be found as the Broncos quietly exited their team hotel on a snowy Monday morning, Feb. 3.

Whereas, John Elway, the Broncos' football boss, said goodbye to several of his key players, and hello to others, as he set out to give the Super Bowl another try in 2014.

This book is about All Things Broncos. Readers will learn details of the down-and-out beginning when the Broncos were an inept laughing sock – the mustard-and-brown vertical stripes were an appropriate look for a Broncos' team that did not post a winning record until its 14th season.

But maybe because of that early suffering, the natural balance of football allowed the Broncos to evolve into an NFL crown jewel – in the 38 years since the start of the 1976 season, the Broncos have only had six losing seasons.

Ask Detroit Lion fans what they think of a team with only six losing records in 38 years.

This book is both a comprehensive study of the team's history and a detailed account of the historic 2013 season recorded by both quarterback Peyton Manning as an individual and the Broncos' offense as a collection.

1: February 1, 2014
WOODY PAIGE

On a bracing Saturday night in New York City, the top floors and the observatory of the venerable Empire State Building are bathed in orange and blue.

The lights are on for the Denver Broncos.

All that's missing from the spectacular scene up above is a gargantuan gorilla wearing an orange Broncos' jersey and hanging onto the famed skyscraper's spire.

Several minutes later the light show turns green and blue to recognize the Seattle Seahawks.

Indeed, two teams are playing tomorrow in Super Bowl XLVIII.

Down below in mid-Manhattan, there is a conglomeration of colors, as if King Kong's colossal crayon box has been spilled on Times Square – the bright, burnt orange and navy blue of the Broncos' sweatshirts and jerseys on the Broncoids from Denver and the Rocky Mountain West, swarming into the mix with the ocean blue and neon green garb of all the 12th men, women and children from Seattle and the Pacific Northwest. Not to mention the kaleidoscope of yellows, reds, purples, browns, blacks and whites in the signs and billboards and streaming lights and screens of Broadway.

Welcome to the City That Never Sleeps, the night before the first Super Bowl to be played in metropolitan New York/New Jersey.

The area from "Give my regards to Broadway" down to "Remember me to Herald Square" has been transformed into a mosh pit called Super Bowl Boulevard with a concert stage, tents, sideshows, football and fashion fascinations, and masses of people. Not far away Jay Z and Beyoncé are performing at the Super Bowl Eve Extravaganza, and Jay Z is screaming, *this is a rock and roll show, not a board meeting*.

It is 11 p.m., the night is crisp, cold and clear, and I'm a stranger in a strange land– in the tradition of newspaperman Damon Runyon, who had come from Colorado to New York to cover sports, and ended up writing about the characters. Runyon, who once tried and failed to organize a professional baseball team in Pueblo, Colorado, became a success a century ago on these same sidewalks where Broncos' fanatics meander before The Big Game. He created some of the most quintessential New York characters ever written, including Nathan Detroit, who Frank Sinatra played in *Guys and Dolls*.

This year, the Wise Guys and the Beautiful Dolls got lucky: there's no snow.

The NFL, New York, New York, and Newark, New Jersey, fretted and fussed over the potential probability of a snowstorm that would slam the Super Bowl and even, ohmigod, postpone it for a day or two.

Temperatures had sunk below freezing during the week but there was no blizzard. Once there had been an infamous Blackout in New York: now the city feared the Great Whiteout.

With Runyon in mind, I turn my attention to the folks and the freaks out in force. The fans may have taken over Broadway, but New York consumes and thrives. I watch a woman, 80 years old if she's a day, barreling her way through the throngs of fans with such tenacity, she would make Terrell Davis proud. I almost laugh but I'm scared to face her wrath.

Most of the fans mingle; others file into the plays – *Book Of Mormon, Rock Of Ages* and, yes, *Phantom Of The Opera*; some hang out at Guy's American Kitchen & Bar – "Oh, there's Guy Fieri;" others are drinking openly on the street – "Oh, there's the Naked Cowboy;" many wander over to Radio City Music Hall for the NFL Awards presentation – "Oh, there's Aaron Rodgers."

To the north the George Washington Bridge is covered in orange lights to salute the Broncos. To the south, the new World Trade Center's tower, recently erected, has an orange glow.

And to the west, across the Hudson River, and over to a hotel in Newark, the Broncos are in their rooms, mentally preparing.

They had moved from the Grand Hyatt, where they had been staying all week, in an attempt to escape the stalking autograph and photo seekers, the relatives, the media, the hangers-on, the cacophony noise.

It's a Super Bowl ritual for teams to play the game of hideandseek the day prior to playing the game of football. Just before midnight, the Broncos are hooked on the feeling of their childhood night before Christmas, and all through the hotel, not a creature is stirring, not an equipment manager.

Back in Manhattan, I am taking a bite out of the Big Apple, a drink here, a stare there, and from all those I converse with, be they in orange and blue or green and blue, the same questions: "Who you got? What will happen? Why?"

"Broncos," I reply. "Peyton Manning, the offense, the experience, the lack of snow, the proDenver sentiment in the stadium, the Year of the Horse in the Chinese Zodiac."

I head back to the midtown Sheraton, the Super Bowl media headquarters, and sit at the bar. Do we ever really know who's going to win? The Broncos had lost before; the Seahawks had lost before, too.

The Broncos get off to a shaky start. A turnover. A tricky play. A score by Seattle, another score, and another, and another and another. And more. It doesn't seem right. The Broncos are out of rhythm, the Seahawks in sync. I can't see the scoreboard, but I can tell the Broncos are no longer orange and blue. Instead, they are fading to black, and…

I am startled suddenly from sleep. It is only 4:10 a.m.

Just a nightmare.

But I am now looking out the hotel window directly into the darkness of a foreboding warning of things to come.

As the Broncos settled in their Newark hotel, they had no idea what was coming.

2: The Ghost of Super Bowls Past

WOODY PAIGE

Super Bowl XLVIII was my 40th in 14 cities, and everybody's first in New York/New Jersey.

Only three sportswriters have witnessed all 48. There had been five before Bob Oates, former writer for the *Los Angeles Times*, died at 93 in 2009. This year the 85-year-old Edwin Pope, former sports editor and daily columnist for *The Miami Herald*, missed his first. According to what I was told at MetLife Stadium, the *Herald* decided not to send Pope, who still writes a number of columns annually from major events, and he declined an offer from the Dolphins to pay for his trip. Although never at a loss for words, the Pope of Miami declined to comment publicly. We last talked at length at last year's Super Bowl in New Orleans. I missed him this year, just as I missed Jim Murray and Red Smith and Furman Bisher and the other greats of the business.

The three who made it to their 48th Super Bowl are all giants of sportswriting: Jerry Green, Jerry Izenberg, and Dave Klein.

Izenberg and Klein are both retired from the Newark *Star-Ledger*, and neither could have ever believed that a Super Bowl would come to their home state. Izenberg now lives in Nevada but returned for the game, and Klein, who owns a website called E-Giants, only had to travel a few miles.

Green (who is retired from the *Detroit News* and lives in California) and I talked in the pressbox for a half hour before the game. "I wonder sometimes who will be the last one standing," said Green, who has been inducted into the Pro Football Hall of Fame. "I never would have believed when I went to the first NFL-AFL championship game (it wasn't called the Super Bowl until later) that there would be 50 of these someday, and I might make it to all of them."

Jerry preferred to talk about the day in Arizona when I persuaded him to join me in a trip to watch parts of six different spring training baseball games. "The games were fine. It was you making me eat a hotdog at every game that got to me." (I wanted to find the best hot dog.)

Then he added, "You and I are among the few who will see the Broncos in all seven of their Super Bowls, and watch them win their third tonight."

He and I were both wrong about who would win No. 48.

I have watched nine Super Bowls in New Orleans (the Broncos twice) – and most every veteran columnist I know agrees with me that every Super Bowl should be in New Orleans. The city that experienced so many lows with Katrina could use more highs, and New Orleans certainly knows how to throw a party. I've been to probably 15 Sugar Bowls and BCS Championship games, a half dozen Mardi Gras, a bunch of Saints games and even a Republican National Convention. I covered Archie Manning playing for the Saints when young Cooper and Peyton were running around. Once Cooper and Peyton even put paper bags scribbled with "Ain'ts" over their heads, which made their father laugh.

New Orleans has the aging but renovated dome daddy stadium, the hotels, the restaurants, the bars, the French Quarter, the Garden District, the river boat trips on the Mississippi, the good people and the good times.

I've been to Miami-Ft. Lauderdale and the Orange Bowl, and the successor stadium, for seven Super Bowls, the Rose Bowl in Pasadena for five Super Bowls, several Rose Bowls and a World Cup Final, and San Diego (3), Tampa (3), Phoenix (3), Atlanta (2), Detroit (2), Minneapolis (1), Jacksonville (1), Houston (1), Indianapolis (1) and San Francisco (Stanford Stadium) for one.

I covered Super Bowls in the 1970s, 80s, 90s, 2000s and 10s. Five decades, 18 different stadiums, a whole lot of teams.

My most memorable early on, as I told Green, was Super Bowl X in the old Orange Bowl because it was such a classic with the Steelers beating the Cowboys, 21-17, and even more so because the movie *Black Sunday* was being filmed during the game. For those who don't remember, the plot was about terrorists trying to blow up the Orange Bowl during the Super Bowl with a bomb in the Goodyear Blimp.

Even though the packed stadium at the Orange Bowl was unaware of the filming of *Black Sunday*, we knew what was going on in the press box. I watched as actor Robert Shaw (*Jaws*) raced down the stadium stairs to get to the field to stop the attackers. He was blocked by an usher, but showed him, I suppose, a TV or media pass, and he was permitted to jump over the sideline wall. You can see it in the movie, if you're ever so inclined. The blimp floated down near the stadium. In the movie, spoiler alert, the blimp actually knocks over a light standard and does land on the field while the Steelers and Cowboys are playing.

In the movie, the day and the game and all the people are saved.

In the book, the blimp, if I remember correctly, actually hit the press box and killed all the sportswriters which would have been met with cheers, I'm sure, by the crowd and America.

The Broncos battled through 7 magnificent Super Bowls. Well, at least 2 were magnificent.

The others were grand for the journey to get there, but not super-lative in the end. The Broncos lost Nos. 1, and 2, 3, and 4, won 5 and 6, and lost No. 7, becoming one of only four teams to appear in at least 7 Super Bowls, and the only team in NFL history to lose five.

The first one, it is claimed, is the best in life and there's still some-thing special about Super Bowl XII – the Broncos' first. Let Terry Bradshaw explain. After the Broncos beat the Pittsburgh Steelers for their first playoff victory, on Christmas Eve, 1977, I rushed into the Steelers' locker room and talked to Bradshaw (who would win four Super Bowls and go on to a pretty nice broadcasting career). The Steelers' down-home quarterback, always talkative and truth-ful, even in defeat, told me, "Be sure to write that everybody should enjoy this ride. If the Broncos do get to the Super Bowl, it will never be like this again. I can promise you that the first one is the best."

I agree. I've been there for all seven and I keep coming back to the first. It was never quite like that again. You were right, Terry.

Here's a look at The Magnificent 7, Yul Brynner, although Broncos Country would rather forget several. This chapter is written totally from memory. I thought it would be better as a stream of conscious-ness and I wonder, actually, how much I do remember and what I want to hang onto.

Super Bowl XII, Jan. 15, 1978, New Orleans Superdome, Dallas Cowboys 27, Denver Broncos 10

The Orange Crush defense vs. the Doomsday defense.

Two nights before the Super Bowl, after I had dinner in the French Quarter, I walked out into the street and saw Coach Landry waiting for the valet to bring his car. First, I was surprised to see the famed and stoic Cowboys coach standing with his wife, with nobody sur-rounding them. Second, I was surprised to see him in the French Quarter on a Friday night before his team played. But I thought about how I'd heard that Landry always went home, even during the season, at dinner time and made his assistants leave the training facility at dark. Unlike coaches who slept on the sofas in their offices, he wanted a home life. And here Landry was, enjoying his wife and a life.

"Coach, I'm Woody Paige and I cover the Broncos and write a column for the *Rocky Mountain News*, and I wanted to say hello."

"I know who you are. I can read."

"I just want to wish you well in the game."

"And the Broncos, too," he said. "I respect their defense and you know I have a special feeling for your quarterback, Craig (Morton). I think it will be a good game. Don't you think it's rather strange that we played the Broncos in the last regular-season game (winning 14-6)?"

I nodded, then said, "I know you won't tell me your game plan, and I wouldn't ask, but in your Super Bowls you always do a couple of weird plays at the beginning and later in the game. I assume you're going to do that again?"

His car pulled up. Landry tugged on his hat, a constant companion, and got into the driver's seat.

He rolled down the window, looked at me, smiled and winked.

The old coach was saying that the Broncos should be ready.

After years of ineptness, the Broncos finally had reached the promised land. Were they staying in a luxurious hotel on Canal or Bourbon Street, or maybe in *a house in New Orleans they call The Rising Sun*, as Eric Burdon of The Animals once sang? *It's been the ruin of many a poor boy...*

No, they were in a dump motel just off the highway on the way into town from the airport. "You got to come look in my room. There's a cockroach that's the size of an offensive guard," linebacker Tom Jackson told me. "This is our reward for reaching the Super Bowl."

I drove past the old motel a year ago while back in New Orleans for another Super Bowl – the night the lights went out in New Orleans and delayed the game for more than a half hour – and thought even with a name change and a paint job, it looked like the same crappy place where the Broncos were stuck in 1978.

Stuck, for sure. Eight Broncos were stuck in the elevator for more than an hour one day leading up to the Super Bowl. Nowadays, Super Bowl teams are housed at the Hyatt or Four Seasons. Back then, the lobby at the Broncos' Super Bowl lodging was barely bigger than that elevator. "It's like going to heaven and finding out it's hell," one player told me. "My dorm room in college was nicer than this."

At least the Superdome was more pleasant – before the game. With about 25,000 Broncos fans on hand, the team came out for warm-ups, and backup lineman Glenn Hyde was honoring the old-time Broncos. He wore the franchise original (and dreadful) yellow–and–brown striped socks. General manager Fred Gehrke had replicas made of the sad socks the first Broncos had worn, and burned, in the franchise's beginning. But only Hyde had the courage to wear them onto the field. He removed them before the game.

On the Cowboys' first offensive play, Landry called a double reverse. Receiver Butch Johnson (who would later play for the Broncos) fumbled the handoff, but recovered.

I wondered if that was what the coach's wink on Friday night meant, or even if Landry had run the play for me. Nah.

In the fourth quarter Staubach handed off to running back Robert Newhouse, who threw a pass in the end zone for a touchdown. What I learned later was that when Newhouse was informed the Cowboys were going to run that play, he tried to get the stick-um stuff off his hands with a towel. Nobody in the entire stadium, especially the Broncos, recognized what he was doing. But I knew Landry had pulled out another of the Super Bowl trick plays that he diagrammed in practice to relax his team. Wink, wink.

Earlier, Staubach threw to Johnson, who made a fingertip catch in the end zone, then fumbled after he hit the ground. In today's NFL, he wouldn't have completed the play, and there would have been no touchdown.

In the second half Craig Morton almost threw an interception.

It would have been his fifth interception.

Morton was the only QB in Super Bowl history with a 0.00 passer rating. Really. I don't have to look it up.

I had asked Craig before the trip to New Orleans if he would keep an oral diary for me. I was writing a book I intended to title "Symphony in Orange" (the publishers hated that title; it became *Orange Madness* instead). Craig, surprisingly, agreed to do it, and I gave him a tape recorder and tapes labeled for each night.

A couple of weeks after the Super Bowl, I hesitantly called Craig and said I'd like the tapes back, to include in the book. He wanted to see me to talk, he said. When we met at a restaurant in Denver's Cherry Creek, Craig had no tapes with him. "I never want them to be used," he said.

"I understand, but what difference does it make? It's an oral history."

After an hour or so, a very reluctant Morton went to his car to get the tapes, but said, "You can listen, but you can't print what I don't want you to."

The first night in New Orleans Morton had said into the recorder, "We did a weigh-in. Tom Glassic (the starting left guard) weighs 219 pounds. He's had a dental problem and couldn't eat. He's lost 40 pounds. No way can he stop the Dallas defensive line. I'm fucked."

Morton knew he had no chance. This would be Doomsday for Denver. It was.

Ed "Too Tall" Jones, Jethro Pugh, Randy White, and Harvey Martin ate the Broncos' offensive line, and Morton was doomed. He didn't finish the game. White and Martin were named co-MVPs of the game.

Why, then, is the memory so meaningful?

Because Denver had endured all those awful seasons and all the terrible games, and the Broncos and their fans deserved to experience the Super Bowl, at least once.

So what if they lost? It was a party in Nawlins. It was a party all season.

Super Bowl XXI, Sunday, Jan. 25, 1986 Pasadena, Calif., Rose Bowl, New York Giants 39, Denver Broncos 20

This one is not quite what it seems in retrospect. The Broncos could have won.

The Broncos would pull off one of the great rallies in playoff history by driving 98½ yards to manage to tie, win and drive to the Super Bowl. The Broncos got the ball on their two-yard line, trailing by seven, with time running down in the fourth quarter. Guard Keith Bishop, now the Broncos' director of security, and then a "bodyguard" for Elway on and off the field, told the offense in the huddle, "We've got them right where we want them." Everybody seemed to relax. Hell, it's only a game.

I asked Elway if the game sped up then. "No, it actually slowed down. When I completed a couple of passes, the crowd quieted, and the Browns seemed shocked. I knew we had a chance." The Broncos would score on an Elway-to-Mark Jackson pass to tie the game. "I knew then we would win it," Elway told me. The Broncos won on a field goal in overtime.

The Super Bowl didn't have the same positive ending, though.

The Broncos led 3-0 early on a Rich Karlis field goal, then 10-7 on a John Elway four-yard run. Then they reached the Giants' 1-yard line and, in three plays, lost five yards. Karlis missed a field goal. He had the distinction of the Super Bowl's longest field goal made (48 yards) and shortest field goal missed (23 yards).

Instant replay was used for the first time in a Super Bowl with a wrong decision. It was determined later by another TV angle Clarence Kay actually had possession of a pass for Denver. Elway was trapped in his end zone for a safety.

There would be another important safety for the Broncos in another Super Bowl...

The Broncos still led 10-9 and got to the Giants' 20-yard line just before halftime. But Karlis missed again.

Last year, before the Super Bowl between Baltimore and San Francisco, Elway and I talked about the five Super Bowls he played in. "That's the one we should have won," he said simply. "It got away from us in the first half."

The Broncos could have been up 21-7 at halftime.

In the second half, with Giants quarterback Phil Simms on target (he would finish 22 of 25 for 268 yards and three touchdowns) and using a flea-flicker for a score, New York scored four touchdowns and a field goal in their first five possessions of the second half, and the Broncos were scorched. Elway threw for 308 yards and was the leading rusher for the Broncos with 29 yards.

That game attracted the largest crowd, until then, in Super Bowl history, and there seemed to be 200,000 people from New York on the grounds around the Rose Bowl during the day.

But Elway was a fisherman with a tale afterward. That one did get away.

Super Bowl XXII, Sunday, Jan. 31, 1987 San Diego, Jack Murphy Stadium, Washington Redskins 42, Denver Broncos 10

On the Broncos' first offensive play, John Elway threw a pass to the wide-open Rick Nattiel for a 57-yard touchdown only 1:57 into the game. It was the quickest touchdown in Super Bowl history. The Broncos would add a field goal in the first quarter and lead 10-0.

"I'm thinking at that point that we can win," Elway told me. The Broncos looked and were playing confident, and the Washington Redskins seemed the team out of sorts.

For the second time, the Broncos had a lead after the first quarter.

"Then, 19 plays later, we're down 39-10. That momentum swing just overwhelmed," Elway told me in 2013. "I'll say this. We didn't quit at halftime. We kept playing hard. We couldn't stop the running game. And we didn't have any answer on offense to slow them down, either."

With Doug Williams, the first African-American quarterback to win a Super Bowl, Washington scored three touchdowns in the second quarter.

At halftime I walked out into the parking lot, and an ambulance was pulling up to a man in a Broncos' jersey lying on the asphalt. The emergency workers covered him with a blanket.

The Broncos' fan had died of a heart attack.

The game didn't seem so important anymore. The Broncos lost again.

But this wouldn't be the last time the Broncos would play a Super Bowl in San Diego.

Super Bowl XXIV, Sunday, Jan. 28, 1989, New Orleans, Superdome, San Francisco 49ers 55, Denver Broncos 10.

This was the match made in heaven for the NFL – John Elway vs. Joe Montana. It turned out to be the matchup from hell for the Broncos.

The 49ers scored on six of their first eight possessions, and Elway, who had willed his Broncos to three Super Bowls in four seasons, couldn't do anything about it. As he told me recently, and I feel the same way, the 49ers and the game were a blur. Jerry Rice caught three touchdown passes from Montana in what still remains the most lopsided Super Bowl ever.

"We can make all the excuses we want to," Elway said last year while he lounged on the beach in Hawaii, reflecting on all his Super Bowls. "But, to me, that was the best football team I ever played against in the Super Bowl. I remember the whole week leading up to it we were concentrating on covering the post (route) on the backside. We didn't do it in the game. Jerry Rice scored three on the post on the backside. No matter what you say about that, No. 1, we didn't play well, and, No. 2, they were a much better team. I was 29. I wasn't thinking I wouldn't get another opportunity, but I was wondering the way the (losing) trend was going, if we would ever figure out a way to play better in these games and win one."

Super Bowl XXXII, Sunday, Jan. 25, 1998, San Diego, Qualcomm Stadium, Denver Broncos 31, Green Bay Packers 24

If you thought Montana vs. Elway was good, how about Elway vs. Brett Favre? But the MVP was a man who was blind for part of the game. Terrell Davis, who had a history of serious migraine headaches, forgot before the game to take the medication that controls the ailment, and he told the Broncos' trainer in the second quarter he was having serious vision issues. Steve Antonopoulos relayed that information to coach Mike Shanahan, who said shortly after to Terrell, "I need you to go back in." Terrell told Shanahan he couldn't see. "I don't need you to see. I just need you to carry out the fake."

On the play Elway faked to Davis and ran the ball in for a touchdown that gave Denver a 14-7 lead.

This would turn out to be one of the greatest Super Bowls in the game's history. The Broncos led 17-14 at halftime and 24-17 after three quarters.

"I've thought lately about Baltimore getting to the Super Bowl (last year). That's the way we did it. You go on the road (in the playoffs), and I think it toughens you as a team," Elway said. After beating Jacksonville at home (to revenge a terrible upset the year before), the Broncos would win at Kansas City (14-10) and Pittsburgh (24-21) to get to this Super Bowl. "You kind of create an 'us against the world' mentality. We had a mindset we weren't going to get beat even though we were two-touchdown underdogs to the Packers."

The atmosphere in Jack Murphy Stadium was electrifying. Favre and Elway were bringing it. I kept thinking in the pressbox that the last team with the ball would win it. As usual, I wasn't quite correct.

Davis would be taken into the locker room, given his medication at halftime, and calmed. He would come back in the third quarter and end up carrying 30 times for 157 yards and three touchdowns.

The Packers, who had won the Super Bowl the year before, scored to tie the game at 24 early in the fourth quarter on a touchdown pass by Favre. "When we got the ball back, we went on a drive and got deep in their territory, and the Packers called a timeout. I went to the sideline and told Mike (Shanahan) and Kube (his former backup and current offensive coordinator Gary Kubiak) that Green Bay couldn't stop us. I felt like, unlike those other Super Bowls, we weren't going to let this one get away from us.

"I wanted to sneak the ball down to the 1-yard line and force the Packers to use another timeout. That idea was shot down. On the next play Terrell just walked in."

He could have crawled in. For the first, and last time, in a Super Bowl, one team let the other team score a touchdown. Elway and the Broncos didn't realize it, but the Packers gave up on the Davis play.

What wasn't known until later was Packers coach Mike Holmgren ordered his defense to let the Broncos score so the Packers would have a chance to tie or win. The first part of Holmgren's rather brilliant strategy succeeded. The Packers would save time and get the ball back with that chance.

With 1:45 to go, the Packers started to race toward the Broncos' end. They got to the 35. Favre completed a short pass, but missed on two. One should have been caught at the 15. On the play, two defensive backs, including AllPro safety Steve Atwater, collided on third down and had to be helped off the field. On fourth down Favre's pass was batted down by the Broncos. And the Broncos would win.

"That was one of the greatest defensive calls in Broncos history," Elway tells me. "Our defense blitzed Favre with two defensive backs, so he couldn't run around the field until he found somebody open. He had to throw in a hurry, and he didn't complete it. That defensive play is overlooked from the game.

"We won the game, something I'd been waiting for my entire life. That was the ultimate moment and memory in my career with the Broncos.

"I've never had another feeling of gratification like that."

A few minutes later, Pat Bowlen, celebrating his first Super Bowl victory as Broncos owner, took the Vince Lombardi Trophy, held it high and blared, "This one's for John." He handed it to Elway.

On the sideline I handed out preprinted fake special edition copies of *The Denver Post* to the players and coaches, who held them up for the TV camera and photographers. Earlier in the week I had written a column covering the front page saying the Broncos had won a Super Bowl, at last. The headline said only: "CHAMPS!" For once, it was true.

After all the years of suffering with a terrible team, then four losses in Super Bowls, the Broncos finally felt the ecstasy.

A couple of hours later back at the hotel (unlike the first time, the Broncos were now staying at a luxurious resort) the band played on and the Broncos partied like rock stars. Back in Denver an entire city celebrated as church bells downtown rang, and people strolled in

LoDo acting loco. Thousands of wild and crazy fans were partying on Larimer Street.

I sat quietly in a corner at the Broncos' party, sipping on a beer, saluting the city and Elway in my own way.

Super Bowl XXXIII, Sunday, Jan. 31, Ft. Lauderdale, Pro Player Stadium, Denver Broncos 34, Atlanta Falcons 19

John Elway and Mike Shanahan against Dan Reeves.

Now there were two for Elway.

"It never entered my mind to walk away after the Super Bowl the year before," Elway says 15 years later. "We still had a very good team coming back. So retiring had never gotten to the serious level. The team for my last Super Bowl actually was the best one I ever played for. I was 37, and I still had a lot of football left in me. Look at the situation and how it all came around. Playing Atlanta and Dan, and what we had and all the issues Mike and I had with him, and how it set up. The situation was made for a perfect ending. We won the game and I could now walk away on top." Elway was named MVP.

At the beginning of May, I was in San Jose covering an Avalanche-Sharks playoff series and Elway was playing in a golf tournament at Cypress Point on the Monterrey Peninsula. I drove over and actually walked up to the 18th green just as he was walking off after he finished his round. Limping off. He certainly was surprised. I asked about his game and how his knee was. He said neither was very good.

Then I asked, "Are you going to retire? My sources tell me you are."

His reply was, "I just don't want to go through rehabilitation (on his injured knee) again. It's time."

After my column came out in The *Post* the next day, Elway officially would make his retirement announcement.

But Elway wasn't finished going to the Super Bowl with the Broncos.

Super Bowl XLVIII, Sunday, Feb. 3, East Rutherford, N.J., MetLife Stadium, Seattle Seahawks 43, Denver Broncos 8

After the debacle, which seemed eerily similar to the earlier defeats by the Broncos in Super Bowls, Elway, in the despair of the moment, wasn't about to make a comparison.

"Each is separate."

But a whole lot more on this Super Bowl later...

3: The Birth of Broncos Nation

WOODY PAIGE

Before Peyton Manning's victory in the duel with Tom Brady in the past AFC Championship game in Denver, before Tebow lost to Brady in a playoff game, before Jake Plummer beat Brady in a playoff game, before Coach McDaniels beat his old mentor Coach Belichick, there was a historic game in the long-distance rivalry between the Broncos and the Patriots:

BOSTON (Associated Press), Sept. 10, 1960 – *Denver launched the American Football League on an upset note, beating Boston 13-10 Friday night on a sensational 79-yard punt return by Gene Mingo.*

The tightrope, hula-hipped gallop just inside the chalk stripe in the third period decided the AFL inaugural though it took an unexpectedly tough Denver defense to preserve it.

The Broncos, doormats of the exhibition schedule when they lost all five starts, came alive with the quarterbacking of Frank Tripucka, the ball-carrying of Al Carmichael and Gene Mingo and a rushing wall which hurt Boston's vaunted passing game.

Carmichael scored on another picture play on the opening maneuver of the second period – a 30-yard flat pass from Tripucka. The 21,597 spectators were brought to their feet as Carmichael eluded two defenders, about five yards beyond the line of scrimmage, twisted away from a third and cut back to the left sideline.

Picking up a cordon of blockers, Carmichael was on his way. The only pursuer having a chance to catch the former Southern California and Green Bay Packer ace was erased by Ken Adamson's block at the 30.

Boston scored on a 33-yard field goal by Gino Capalletti in the first period and a 10-yard Tommy Greene to Jim Colclough pass near the end of the third quarter. A 46-yard return of an intercepted pass by Chuck Shonta set up the score.

The first AFL game was played at Boston University Field. The Broncos had previously lost their first exhibition to the same Patriots team, 43-6 in Providence, R.I., before a cozy gathering of 4,706.

Mingo (who didn't attend college, but served in the military and played on a U.S. Navy base team before begging for a tryout in a letter to the Broncos) also kicked an extra point, becoming the first African-American placekicker in the AFL or the National Football League.

Tripucka, a former NFL and Canadian Football League quarterback, had begun the 1960 season with the Broncos as an offensive assistant coach. Because the Broncos' original quarterback tryouts were so inept, even awful, head coach Frank Filchock persuaded Tripucka to come out of retirement and play again. He ended up as the starting quarterback for more than three seasons.

Tripucka wore No. 18, which was retired in his honor. Later his number was unretired when Peyton Manning joined the Broncos in 2012. Manning asked the elderly and ailing Tripucka if it would be OK if he wore the same number as the Broncos' first quarterback. When Tripucka died in September of 2013, Manning visited his sons in New Jersey the day before the Giants–Broncos game and paid his respects to the Broncos' first quarterback.

Carmichael would go on to become a famous actor and author in California.

The reason why this was the AFL's inaugural game? The rest of the league's opening games were played later in the weekend.

The Broncos would win three of their first four, and four of six in the regular season, and would seem to be a contender in the upstart league. They finished the 1960 season with a 4-10 record, so the start was a bit misleading.

They would play in several of the most famous stadiums in the country: the Polo Grounds (the old home of baseball's New York Giants), Candlestick Park (the new home of the San Francisco Giants), the Los Angeles Coliseum (former Olympics venue and then the home stadium of the Los Angeles Chargers), the Cotton Bowl (home of the Dallas Texans) and Buffalo's War Memorial Stadium (later the baseball stadium for the movie *The Natural*).

The Broncos' home games were at Bears Stadium, an old garbage dump west of downtown that had been transformed into a minor-league baseball park. It was not suitable for football. In fact, the Denver Bears baseball team got first scheduling rights, so the Broncos played all their exhibitions and their early regular-season games on the road the first few seasons. The Broncos had to wait to play at home until after baseball season, when temporary stands could be erected on the east side.

The Bears were more important than the Broncos.

But the stadium did have an impressive, large South Stands section.

And therein lies the tale of the reason Denver got a professional football team in the first place.

In 1948, young Bob Howsam and his family owned a Western League baseball franchise in Denver and decided to replace the old baseball park on South Broadway (where a Sam's Club and K-Mart now are located) with a new stadium, near downtown. They purchased a landfill and constructed a modern, sparkling 18,000-seat edifice, originally called Cold Stadium (appropriately). The very successful Bears (Howsam was named minor league executive of the year twice) became a Triple A affiliate of the Yankees and the Pirates in the 1950s, and Howsam became friends with baseball legend Branch Rickey, who was responsible for bringing Jackie Robinson to the Brooklyn Dodgers as the first African-American in Major League Baseball.

Because of baseball expansion to the West Coast, Rickey planned in the late 1950s to start another "major" league to compete with the American and National Leagues. Howsam wanted Denver to have one of the eight proposed teams in the new Continental League. Rickey said, however, that the ballpark, now Bears Stadium, needed to be enlarged to at least 25,000 seats. So Howsam hired a local contracting company owned by the Phipps brothers, Gerald and Allan, members of a famous and rich Colorado family (which owned the Phipps Mansion near Cherry Creek and the Phipps Ranch, which is now the booming Highlands Ranch housing community south of Denver).

The South Stands added 8,000 seats to the stadium, but a serious problem developed. Major League Baseball thwarted The Continental League by awarding expansion teams to two of its intended areas– New York (Mets) and Houston (Colt 45s)– and moving the Washington Senators to a third – Minneapolis, St. Paul. A future Major League franchise was promised to Denver but there was no timetable, and it wouldn't be soon (the promise was broken by baseball authorities, although Denver eventually would receive an expansion team more than 30 years later).

Howsam was stuck with a bill for the South Stands, a section he didn't need for minor-league baseball. So he decided to join the new football league. Rather than pay the Phipps for the South Stands construction, Howsam, who was in debt after paying $125,000 to the fledgling AFL, negotiated a deal to give them a minority share of the ownership.

"I was a baseball guy but I was about to become a football guy, too, because I needed to pay off the South Stands and figure out a way to fill them."

Suddenly, Howsam was involved in pro football.

Chicago, Aug. 14, 1959 (Associated Press) — A second professional football league, the American Football League, was formally organized today.

Lamar Hunt, of Dallas, said the league will begin play in 1960 with teams in Los Angeles, New York, Denver, Dallas, Houston and Minneapolis-St. Paul.

Representatives of the six sites [including Howsam] met in Chicago to discuss such matters as player draft, league constitution, by-laws and working agreements.

The group hopes to have draft plans in operation by this fall to provide players for the new loop.

Hunt announced two weeks ago the league would be formed. He said each team probably will play 14 league games and four exhibitions.

Lamar Hunt was son of Texas billionaire oilman H.L. Hunt. With his inherited wealth, he decided he wanted to own a profession football team and become a sportsman in Dallas. When the elder Hunt was told that Lamar could lose a million dollars a year on this football venture, H.L. said, "Well that means he can only last 100 years or so at it."

Hunt was the catalyst. When the NFL wouldn't award Dallas an expansion team, he recruited several other very wealthy men, including Houston oil man Bud Adams and hotelier Baron Hilton, to join the enterprise to create a rival football league to the NFL. The original organizational meeting was held in Chicago in 1959, and included six potential cities for the American Football League– Dallas, Denver (Bob Howsam), Los Angeles (Hilton), Houston (Adams), New York and Minneapolis.

Before the league could officially organize, however, the NFL decided to put an expansion franchise in Minneapolis (1960) and later in Dallas. So the AFL added Buffalo, Boston, and Oakland.

The original AFL owners were called "The Foolish Club." Ralph Wilson, the owner of the Buffalo Bills, died March 25, 2014, leaving Baron Hilton as the only original owner from the AFL still alive. Lamar Hunt died in 2006.

Howsam was the owner in Denver – along with the Phipps brothers, who took a piece of the franchise instead of payment for their South Stands construction and the temporary stands they would erect each year to make the stadium capacity 34,000.

The Denver franchise didn't have the funds of the other owners, but the Broncos did get a piece of the $10 million TV deal struck with ABC, and that allowed Howsam to start doing business.

Denver didn't seem to care. The Dusty Old Cowtown, which was raised out of the dirt at the base of the Rocky Mountain during a gold rush in the 1850s (Pike's Peak or Bust!), wasn't much interested in professional football, or even college football, for that matter. The University of Denver had a team and a stadium on University Boulevard (which served as a home for the Broncos on occasion) and the University of Colorado had been sometimes successful, but people in Denver in 1960 seemed more interested in the annual Stock Show and Rodeo and an AAU basketball tournament that came to town annually, not to mention figuring out how to grow into a city.

The two Denver newspapers paid little attention to the new football team, and the Broncos were generally referred to as "Howsam's Folly."

The team's name came out of a contest that was virtually ignored. Out of 500 entries, 7 of them were for the Broncos, which had been the name of the town's Midwest Baseball League team in 1921. A name was drawn from those 7 entries, and the winner of the contest was Ward Vining of Lakewood, a Denver suburb. He was director of Title 1 for the Colorado Department of Education. Ward got 2 season tickets and assorted other team memorabilia. Reserved seat tickets for the 1960 season were available at $4.50 per ti ket per game, so the value of 2 season tickets was $72.

In the role of general manager, Howsam hired Dean Griffing, executive director of the Optimist Bowl. In 1958 the Tucson Optimist Club pitted the All-American team seniors against a team of All-Americans from smaller schools. The bowl didn't last long. Griffing, who had played at Kansas State and then was a linebacker, a coach and a general manager in the Canadian Football League, named Filchock, also a former CFL coach, as his head coach.

Griffing, known for his frugality (the real reason Howsam hired him), is mostly remembered for buying old uniforms from the defunct Copper Bowl. The team colors were gold and what the players called "barnyard brown." He also outfitted the team in vertically striped yellow-and-brown socks. The Broncos were a laughingstock show that looked like it belonged in a clown car.

"Those socks that were striped with mustard and shit colors were the most ridiculous things I ever saw in my life," said defensive tackle Bud McFadin. Safety Goose Gonsoulin wasn't quite as graphic. "They made you look like a peg. It was unique. Put it that way."

After extra points and field goals sailed into the South Stands, Griffin, who would be standing in the section, would fight with the few fans over possession of the football.

The Broncos' first home game attracted 18,372 (although many years later, hundreds of thousands would claim they were at the game) and the last home game of the season against the New York Titans drew 5,861.

Not an auspicious season to start with.

But the Broncos did beat the Patriots in the opening game and Denver did have a professional football team.

Howsam didn't last long as owner. He sold the team to a group headed by Cal Kunz the next year, and the Phipps brothers would end up with 42%. Griffin and Filchock were fired.

Howsam would go on to become the architect of "The Big Red Machine" Cincinnati Reds dynasty and a powerful Major League executive. He ultimately returned to Colorado in retirement and died in Glenwood Springs.

4: Fasten Your Seatbelts, It's Going to be a Bumpy Night

WOODY PAIGE

The Broncos almost didn't survive the early going. In 1965 voters turned down a bond project to build a new stadium (the architectural plans were sold to San Diego and used for its new stadium, which still is in use in an expanded state today– although the Chargers have sought a new stadium for years).

Without a new stadium, the team was losing considerable money. Offers came in from Atlanta, Phoenix, and even Chicago and Philadelphia (which already had NFL teams), and the Broncos almost moved to Birmingham. The Broncos wouldn't be able to join in the merger with the NFL without 50,000 seats. So, several local leaders, urged on by Charlie Goldberg, raised half a million dollars to add new seats on the east side of the stadium.

The stadium capacity was increased to 50,000 with a permanent three-deck section that was, in a novel way, moved by water flotation between the football and baseball configurations. In a few years the stadium added higher decks on the west and north sides and could hold 75,000. And the name was changed to Mile High Stadium.

Gerald and Allen Phipps agreed to buy the rest of the ownership for $1.25 million (after rejecting a $4 million offer from Atlanta businessmen).

The Phipps seemed to be making a foolish decision, but they would eventually realize about 30 times their investment when they sold the franchise in the 1980s.

And they had saved the Broncos from vacating Denver.

The Broncos were the first team to win an AFL game back in 1960. In 1967, they would have another major accomplishment.

The NFL and the AFL reached an agreement in 1966 to merge by 1970, and the two leagues would play their first championship game on Jan. 15, 1967. Green Bay would whip the Chiefs 35-10.

The Broncos of the AFL and the Detroit Lions of the NFL scheduled an exhibition in Denver (at the University of Denver Stadium) on Aug. 5, 1967. Lions defensive tackle Alex Karras, who would go on to become more famous as a Monday Night Football analyst and as the *Blazing Saddles* movie character 'Mongo,' vowed that if the Lions lost in Denver, he would walk back to Detroit.

The Broncos became the first AFL team to beat an NFL team, even if it was just an exhibition, 13-7. Karras quietly flew back to Detroit.

Even though the Broncos were pitiful most seasons, the people filled up the place, and a sellout streak began in 1970 which now extends through 44 seasons, the second longest in the NFL after Washington. Since the merger, the Broncos have never experienced a non-sellout game.

After losing $400,000 in 1960, the Broncos soon became a break-even proposition; then a money-maker for the Phipps, especially as franchise values rose significantly.

Yet, on the field, the Broncos weren't much. In the beginning, they drafted from college magazines. In the battle against the NFL, they couldn't sign draft picks. One pick named Dick Butkus chose the Chicago Bears over the Broncos. Really?

They finally signed a No. 1 pick in 1967 when Syracuse running back Floyd Little joined the team. He wound up in the Pro Football Hall of Fame.

Veteran pro and college coach Lou Saban (who was on the losing side as head coach of the Boston Patriots in that game with the Broncos in 1960) was hired to run the team and the organization in 1967. He gave the Broncos a true professionalism and a competitive team, even if it didn't reach the postseason or even a .500 mark.

Fans and lapdog newspaper and TV media in Denver who had been patient and polite started to become needy and nasty after Saban had four losing seasons, then the "half a loaf" game against the Miami Dolphins brought everything to a head. In the 1971 opener at Mile High Stadium, the score was tied at 10 late when the Broncos got the ball for a last time with timeouts left in their pocket. Saban chose to run out the clock rather than try to go for a winning field goal. Afterward, he claimed "half a loaf is better than none." That turned out to be the end for Saban. He resigned when the Broncos were 2-6-1.

John Ralston was lured away from Stanford for the 1972 season to be the Broncos' coach and general manager. He had turned Stanford into a national power, winning consecutive Pac-8 championships and Rose Bowls over Big Ten champions Ohio State and Michigan, both undefeated, in 1970-71. Stanford quarterback Jim Plunkett was awarded the Heisman Trophy in 1970.

Considered a brilliant recruiter, Ralston proved to be just as productive as a draft manager, selecting 13 players in the next five drafts that would become starters and/or Pro Bowl choices. Among that group were linebackers Randy Gradishar and Tom Jackson, cornerbacks Louis Wright and Steve Foley, running back Otis Armstrong, tight end Riley Odoms, and a half dozen offensive and defensive linemen. He acquired five other starters in trades and totally turned over the team and turned it into an AFC West contender.

Ralston was of the Dale Carnegie School of positive thinking. He wrote the goal, *Win 12, go to and win Super Bowl* on an index card and placed it on the dashboard of his car, making sure it was the first thing he looked at and thought about on his way to the Broncos' headquarters each day.

But there were a lot of problems for Ralston to deal with, not the least of which being the fact that the practice field was only 60 yards long. This led to media (me) writing: "That's why the Broncos never have a drive over 60 yards. They don't know what to do with the other 40 yards."

Ralston and I weren't particularly on the same wave length. In 1974 he had his public relations director Bob Peck call and order me to Ralston's office the next day. "I don't work for the team," I told Peck. "He can't order me to do anything. He can *request*."

When I did show up (a few days later) at his office, Ralston said, "Your writing is not the way things are done in Denver. You have to be positive like everyone else in the press."

The Broncos had won five games in 1972 and seven the next season.

"When you start winning a few more games, I'll start being a bit more positive," I told the coach.

The Broncos won seven in 1974. I wasn't much more positive and the coach/GM wasn't much more inclined to talk to me again. In fact, he told Peck the media weren't allowed to fly on the team plane to games anymore. I wasn't popular among my peers.

The Broncos did have promise. What they didn't have was a head coach who was a great coach. As suggested, Ralston was an incredible personnel director, but not much of an X's and O's guy. When I ripped his offensive coordinator Max Coley after six consecutive insipid showings by the offense (no more than 17 points in any of the games), Coley called me one night at home and wanted to have an off-the-record conversation. He said I was right about the offense and he accepted the blame, but that I should know Ralston was trying to run the offense and should stay out of the way because he didn't know what he was doing.

Weird confession by an NFL coordinator.

The Broncos averaged only 18 points a game in that 1975 season. They finished 6-8.

In 1976 the Broncos were sensational on defense, allowing more than 19 points only twice all season. I gave the defense a nickname: "Orange Crush."

The offense was scoring more, as Coley (he informed me) took over as coordinator from Ralston. In fact, the Broncos scored 48 points against the helpless and winless Tampa Bay Buccaneers. Bucs coach John McKay, who had coached at Southern Cal against Ralston at Stanford and Coley at Oregon, wasn't happy when the game ended. He refused to shake hands with Ralston and said he wanted to fight Coley. He accused them of running up the score. A couple of days later McKay called Coley to apologize. He didn't call Ralston.

The Broncos finished 9-5, which was admirable, but they still finished four games behind the Oakland Raiders in the division. There were no wild card teams then, but two other second-place teams in the AFC had better records, anyway.

Despite the best record in the club's history, the Broncos still weren't quite there and I didn't think they would make it with Ralston as the coach. "He should be the general manager and hire someone else to take over on the field," I wrote.

A lot of veteran players agreed with me.

5: Mutiny on the Broncos

WOODY PAIGE

The Broncos won five of their last six games in 1976, but didn't reach the postseason. They never had. And the players, the media, the fans, and the ownership were restless.

Ralston had not fulfilled his objective of winning the Super Bowl, or even the division.

Lyle Alzado, the Wild Man of the Orange Crush defense, told me privately, "We've got to get rid of that son of a bitch."

Safety Billy Thompson said, "John came into a defensive meeting one day, and didn't have any idea what we were doing."

Otis Armstrong told me, "No way we shouldn't have made the playoffs with our team and that schedule."

A number of other players were criticizing Ralston and saying he should be fired.

Despite my recommendation that a new coach be hired and Ralston concentrate on being the general manger, the Phipps Bros. elevated assistant GM Fred Gehrke and announced that Ralston would continue as coach. The two fine gentlemen got it backwards, as I once told Allan Phipps when he invited me to join him for (many) drinks at his exclusive downtown Denver club. "We didn't realize that the players hated John so much. We made a mistake, and we had a mutiny on our hands."

Eight days after the 1976 season ended, just five days before Christmas, 12 Broncos convened in a conference room at the Holiday Inn on Colorado Boulevard in Denver to talk about what they could do about Ralston.

I named them Denver's Dirty Dozen.

"We're too close. We can't let him blow this," one of the players shouted to the others- a mix of veterans and young players, whites and blacks, starters and backups. All lived in Denver in the off-season. They voted unanimously that they wanted Ralston gone and they drafted a statement they would make to selected press the next day. The players got on phones at the hotel (there were no cell phones then) and managed to locate 20 other players to agree to sign the statement.

Before their group press conference (this moment was the most united the Broncos had been in the club's history) they got word from Gerald Phipps and Fred Gehrke that there had to be a meeting. The players decided to wait until after they talked with the two.

Phipps and Gehrke studied the statement and Phipps told the players, "If you will hold off, we'll try to do something. Give us some time. If you read this to the press, you'll be making a mistake we can't undo."

The players called off the press conference.

In the parking lot several handed me a copy of the supposedly confidential statement. "You can say it was leaked to you. You know what to do with this," one player told me.

I said, "This isn't a leak. It's a flood."

The statement read: "We don't believe it is possible to win a championship under the guidance of John Ralston. He has lost the respect of his players, and we don't believe he is capable of coaching us to a championship."

When I printed the statement in the *Rocky Mountain News* the next morning (before there was texting or tweeting), Phipps called

Gehrke, and, according to what Gehrke told me later, said, "I've never seen anything handled so miserably."

John Ralston rushed back from the West Coast to Denver after being read the statement and released one of his own: "Young people are impetuous and make mistakes. I'm not a vindictive person."

Privately, though, Ralston was incensed and told others he would get rid of the ringleaders. One was veteran wide receiver-punter Billy Van Heusen, who was ordered by Phipps to apologize to Ralston personally. Van Heusen told other players, "We made a mistake. He (Ralston) is more determined to keep the job than ever before. That statement has brought management together."

Gerald Phipps was squeezed. A majority of his team's starters had signed a petition to demand Ralston's ouster. There was unbelievable tension. One of the Dirty Dozen players, kicker Jim Turner (who played for Ralston in college) publicly came out in support of the coach and said, "The players were stupid for pulling this stunt."

The club tried to make the matter simmer down but it just continued to boil.

In mid-January Phipps and Gehrke decided that, indeed, Ralston had to go. They told him he could announce he was resigning, and he would be paid the rest of his contract.

Ralston surrendered. His final statement was short and somewhat sweet. "I wish the Broncos all the success in the world." He was bitter, and bolted.

Ralston had almost been too successful with the Broncos. They thought they had a winner. He had raised expectations by telling everybody they would go to and win a Super Bowl. His record in five seasons with the Broncos was 34-33-3. He was the first winning coach the Broncos ever had.

Ralston spent the next year in Denver working out of the office of the Dale Carnegie Associates. He didn't attend games and he didn't get an offer to coach another NFL team ever again. He was an assistant with several pro teams in the NFL and Canada, and coached the Oakland Invaders of the USFL. He became the coach at San Jose State in the 1990s for four years but didn't have a winning season.

This year Ralston will be 87. He has an office on the San Jose State campus and occasionally attends practices. He rarely talks about his years with the Broncos.

The Broncos had experienced the biggest player revolt in pro football history. It was reminiscent of the sailors' mutiny led by Mr. Christian in *Mutiny on the Bounty*.

And the next season, 1977, with new coach Red Miller, the Broncos would fulfill two-thirds of Ralston's dream: they would win 12 and go to the Super Bowl.

6: 1977: From Orange Curse to Orange Crush
WOODY PAIGE

The Broncos' time had come, finally, in 1977.

Orange blended with Red.

Red Miller, a long-time assistant coach (including a stint with the Broncos), was selected to replace John Ralston, and people wondered. Miller had not been a head coach in the NFL and he had not been a popular name in football.

In fact, Miller, who was an offensive line coach with the Patriots, had just about given up coaching, thinking he would never get a chance for a job as a head man. But he made one more push.

Miller was known as a no nonsense coach who believed in a conservative offense and a tough defense. The people in Denver weren't overwhelmed by the choice. When he opened camp in Ft. Collins on the Colorado State University practice field, Miller had brought another touch that confused Broncos backers: he had a popsicle break for the players during workouts.

The Broncos had the "Orange Crush" defense led by coordinator Joel Collier (who had previously coached with Miller) and such players as linebackers Randy Gradishar, Tom Jackson, Bob Swenson and Joe Rizzo, and defensive end Lyle "Wild Man" Alzado and a secondary that included safety Billy Thompson and cornerback Louis Wright.

On the other hand, the offense didn't scare anybody. There were a bunch of guys who could have been named Joe.

But the Broncos made two other major additions on offense in the off-season. They had traded mediocre quarterback Steve Ramsey to the Giants for veteran quarterback Craig Morton, who had started a Super Bowl (and lost) for the Dallas Cowboys and even, one season, alternated every other play with Roger Staubach, before being dumped in favor of Staubach.

Morton was considered a has-been.

The Broncos also brought in free agent Steve Spurrier. Even though Spurrier had been a Heisman Trophy winner at the University of Florida (the Broncos later would have a former Gators' quarterback who had won a Heisman – can you guess his name?), he had been a career backup with the 49ers.

Morton had two awful seasons with the Giants, winning 6 starts and losing 19. I wrote at the time, "The Broncos gave the Giants their bad quarterback in exchange for the Giants' bad quarterback. It was an even deal."

Spurrier had joined the Tampa Bay Bucs the previous season and was the starter in 12 games that the expansion team lost.

This was considered the last chance for both Morton and Spurrier. The Broncos also had quarterbacks Norris Weese (a successor at Ole Miss to Archie Manning and a quarterback in the World Football League) and youngster Craig Penrose.

"If you have two quarterbacks," it is said, "you have none." If you have four, it could be said, you might as well have four dozen.

Only three would make the team. It was assumed that Spurrier or Morton would be one, and Penrose (a passer) and Weese (a scrambler) would end up as reserves.

Morton looked impressive in camp and became the favorite after starting the first two exhibitions.

Spurrier was given the start in Atlanta against the Falcons and he played quite well, despite bruising a knee.

I had known Spurrier since we were high school kids in Tennessee. He was the son of a preacher man in East Tennessee before heading off to Florida. During training camp we sort of hung out, and on team charters we sat together and played backgammon and talked (with deep Southern accents) about football. He was a student of the game, and planned one day to become a coach. "But I want to prove myself as a quarterback, and I can do it here," he told me.

On the late night flight back to Denver from Atlanta, Spurrier asked me, "So, did I do enough to get the starting job?"

I hesitated. "Steve, I've got to tell you the truth. You're not even going to make the team."

He slammed his hand on the backgammon board (he was winning 15 bucks) and replied, "What do you mean?"

"Morton is the starter, and the other two will be kept."

He sat in silence for the rest of the trip. As we landed, he said, "If that's true, I better begin thinking about coaching. But I don't believe it."

The next day he asked Miller for a meeting. When it was over, Spurrier left the Broncos.

He never played another NFL game.

Spurrier eventually would return to the University of Florida as head coach, and win a national championship. He did get back to the NFL, as the head coach with Washington. That was a failure. But Spurrier has turned around the South Carolina program and become legendary as the self-proclaimed Ol' Ball Coach.

Morton was the starter opening Sunday 1977 at home against the St. Louis Cardinals.

The Broncos won 7-0 on a naked bootleg by Morton, who was not a nimble quarterback, the reason nobody would expect him to run.

Many years later Peyton Manning would score a touchdown on the same kind of play and say: "That play works about every five years."

It worked several times in '77 for Morton.

The Broncos would win six in a row, including a 30-7 awe-inspiring victory in Oakland. Late in the game, after the Broncos had intercepted four passes, and even scored on a fake field goal play (a pass from holder Weese to kicker Jim "Hightops" Turner), Broncos linebacker Tom Jackson went over to the Raiders sideline and shouted at coach John Madden, "It's all over, Fat Man."

In reality, it would be.

Even though the Raiders would come back to win in Denver 24-14, the Broncos' devastating defense, which didn't allow more than 14 points in any of the other 13 games in a 14-game season, became the most dominant in the NFL.

The Broncos' defense of 1977 was to football what the Broncos' offense of 2013 became.

They lost only one more regular-season game, the meaningless finale in Dallas, and finished 12-2 and won the franchise's first division title.

The players who had forced John Ralston's removal the year before got the last laugh, and Red Miller proved he belonged as head coach. And Morton, grabbed off the scrap heap, proved he was a legitimate starting quarterback.

The Broncos clinched their first playoffs in Houston, and would host the Pittsburgh Steelers, the Steel Curtain, and quarterback Terry Bradshaw.

Denver had a case of Orange Madness. And when the Broncos upset the Steelers, the town was painted orange, literally. Citizens painted their houses orange or put orange toilet seats in their bathrooms, or painted their bodies orange and did a naked bootleg on Christmas Eve downtown.

The AFC Championship was, appropriately enough, the Broncos vs. the Raiders. Tom Jackson and The Fat Man confronted each other a third time.

Officials failed to make the correct call when Denver running back Rob Lytle fumbled near the goal line, and the Raiders' recovery was disallowed, allowing the Broncos to beat the Raiders 20–17.

It was a happy new year for the Super Broncos. They were going to the Big Game for the first time in team history. Madden and I would have lunch in the circular hotel next to Mile High Stadium in the offseason and when he returned to Denver to visit a longtime friend he said, "We were assaulted in that game and got jobbed. If that fumble was called, we win." He was bitter for a long time– probably until he got a network announcing job. Things worked out well for John Madden.

The Broncos' victory would lead to two changes by the NFL. Nobody knew that Morton had spent most of the week in the hospital with a badly-bruised hip. He didn't practice once. Before the game Miller had to tie Morton's cleats and the coach told the offensive line, "If Craig is sacked even once, he's out of the game." Morton wasn't sacked. The league would demand the next year that teams file an injury report each week, and a pool reporter had to be permitted to watch and report on injuries at every Super Bowl practice.

Tapes showed conclusively that Lytle had fumbled, and the league's competition committee soon began discussing the use of TV replays to determine certain plays. Several years later, that call would have been overturned.

Nevertheless, the Broncos would go on to New Orleans to replay the Cowboys in the Super Bowl.

The Cowboys would win rather easily, but the Broncos had established themselves as a real NFL contender, and would be one of the most successful teams in the league for the next three and a half decades.

7: The Duke of Denver
WOODY PAIGE

The first week of November, 1982, I walked into Dan Reeves' office – back when you didn't need an appointment, or have to wade through secretaries, staff and security – and interrupted the Denver Broncos' coach as he chewed on a submarine sandwich. I wanted him to chew on another subject.

"I have just seen the future of pro football, Dan," I announced proudly.

"What?" he said in that southern accent you could pour on pancakes.

"John Elway."

"Tell me something I don't know. I haven't seen him play in person, and we haven't looked much at his films, but there's no reason to. We're not going to have the first pick in the draft and that's where we'd have to be. Why waste our time?"

"Dan, you should do whatever you can to get this kid. He's going to be a Hall of Fame quarterback and maybe the best ever in the game."

"Well, it ain't happening here."

The last week of January, 2004, I walked into the Pro Football Hall of Fame selection meeting in a conference room at the Houston convention center. As the committee representative from Denver, I prepared to make my nomination speech for John Elway.

Elway had been retired five years, was eligible for induction, and was on the final list of 15 for election. He was a cinch for first ballot, unless, somehow, I screwed it up.

For weeks I had written and rewritten a speech that would be given to the other 35 committee members on the Saturday morning before Sunday's game. Normally a nomination speech lasts at least 10 minutes. The media member from a finalist's city will list statistics of the player and talk about coaches', general managers', and players' evaluations of the nominee. He will give a short bio of the potential Hall of Famer and any other pertinent information (Pro Bowl selections, awards) followed by a passionate plea for the outstanding player to be permanently enshrined in the hallowed hall in Canton, Ohio.

When I stood up and pushed back my chair, I rejected a microphone and said loudly and proudly:

"Gentlemen, John Elway."

Then I sat down.

Everybody in the meeting applauded. I assumed they were giving Elway (who obviously wasn't in the room) a rousing vote of confidence. It was pointed out to me though, by another voter, that the entire committee was thrilled that I had just offered up the shortest nomination speech in the history of the Hall of Fame voting process.

It's difficult to argue that more need be said.

Nobody at the long, rectangular table said anything negative about Elway. That was a rarity in the room; the debate can become rather blistering. Later, after all the nominees had been discussed (some at length), the secret ballots were cast on small pieces of white paper (no new-fangled technical advances for this group) and a national accounting firm's employees (who also served as guards outside the door) tabulated the results. Even though the results are not made public (or even disclosed to the committee members), I'm certain

Elway's selection was unanimous that day. There was no reason for me to sermonize at length. I was preaching to a receptive choir. John Elway was The Natural. He may have been the best quarterback ever to play the game.

In the 22 years between my walking into Reeves' office and walking into the Hall of Fame selection meeting, a lot happened to John Elway and the Denver Broncos.

After he had played for the Broncos several years I nicknamed Elway "The Duke of Denver." He shared the same first name with John Wayne – the original Duke. Wayne and Elway also shared a similar gait – a stiff-backed, bow-legged, toe-to-heal style of walking that makes men seem tougher, more resolved, entering swinging doors of an old-West bar with a purpose. Both didn't just come into a room; they took over the room. They were about the same size, 6-foot-4, and had the same presence. As I used to tell people, you always knew at a crowded party which one was the leader of the pack – a Bill Clinton, a James Earl Jones, a John Wayne, a Bart Starr, and a John Elway.

Wayne and Elway had that swagger, that Elvis smirk, that smile of confidence, that powerful, rugged face and those broad shoulders.

Duke. It was perfect. The other reason I named him after the famed actor was Elway, as Wayne before him, always rode to the rescue at the end of the movie, uh, game. Wayne saved the school marm, the cattle, the sheriff, the whole damn town. He was the real man who shot Liberty Valance. He got the bad guys. Well, Elway always seemed to rescue the Broncos from the men in black. He fired bullets. He made the Dusty Old Cowtown in Colorado happy again. Like Wayne, and unlike Shane, Elway would come back, and the team, and the town would win, and everybody was happy.

The Duke of Denver.

Frank Sinatra was The Chairman of the Board. Brett Favre was the Gunslinger.

John didn't say much publicly about the nickname, but he wore it well, and liked it, as he told friends. Much later, the majority of the memorabilia he signed – $249.95 for a photo – was titled "The Duke of Denver."

The son of college coach Jack Elway, John was always considered a California blond beach boy but he was born in Montana on June 28, 1960. In 1979, after a terrific high school athletic career, he decided to play football and baseball at Stanford.

Even though Stanford compiled a 20-23 record and never played in a bowl while Elway was the starting quarterback for four seasons, he was a consensus All-American, Pac-10 player of the year twice and named later as one of the top 25 college football players of all time. Unlike Tim Tebow, who did win a Heisman Trophy, but like Peyton Manning, Elway finished second in the prestigious trophy's balloting. Peyton probably didn't win because he never beat Florida or won a national championship. John didn't win because he never played in a bowl and didn't win his last game.

In that final game, Stanford-Cal, the Cardinal trailed 19-17 with time running out and the ball on its own 13, fourth and 17. Elway completed a 29-yard pass and drove Stanford to the 35-yard line, where a field goal gave his team the lead with time for only a kickoff return by Cal.

The Bears scored on one of the wackiest plays in college football history. On the kickoff, Cal players lateraled the ball five times (two were later analyzed as illegal forward laterals) and scored when the Stanford Marching Band came on the field prematurely and kept the Cardinal from making a tackle before the touchdown. The play has been replayed on national TV since 1982 thousands of times, and hundreds of other teams have attempted the same kind of wacky play at the end of games, sans band. Few, though, over the years score on the final play.

Elway was very embittered about what occurred and said the officials ruined the end of his career. But, over the years, he has softened his stance, and laughs when he talks about the "Stanford Band" play. Yet, it kept him out of a bowl (Stanford finished 5-5 and didn't qualify) and probably cost him the Heisman.

The consolation prize, though, was that Elway was the logical choice for the first overall pick in the 1983 NFL draft.

The Baltimore Colts owned the selection, and that was a serious problem for Elway.

John's father Jack helped convince John there was no way he should play for Baltimore coach Frank Kush. When Jack Elway and Kush had coached together in a college all-star bowl game, Elway learned first-hand about Kush's disciplinarian coaching style and tactics. Kush had been a successful, but controversial, coach at Arizona State, where he was accused of treating his players as if they were soldiers in boot camp or prisoners at Sing-Sing. He created a "bull in the ring" drill during workouts. One player would be the bull, a teammate would charge him, and they would fight until the whistle blew. Another drill involved the running back going against the entire defense. As in the knife fight in *Butch Cassidy and the Sundance Kid*, there were no rules, and, as another movie title suggested, there would be blood. In pre-season workouts, a player who didn't go full-out was forced to run among the cacti up and down a hill known, not so affectionately, as "Mt. Kush." Ultimately, Kush would be fired after a punter claimed the coach had punched him during a game. The school's internal investigation found Kush had committed too many violations of harassment and bullying of his players.

Kush wound up with the Colts.

Elway representatives told Baltimore owner Bob Irsay that John would not play for Baltimore. If they elected to draft him he would pursue baseball. Elway had played in the off-season in the New York

Yankees organization and even made an appearance in Yankee Stadium, wearing a Yankees uniform, for a batting practice session before one game. The Colts didn't believe the threat or bluff and drafted Elway anyway, No. 1.

He refused to talk to the Colts about a contract, saying it was the West Coast or nothing.

The Colts considered a trade offer from Oakland owner Al Davis, and Elway thought he would end up with the Raiders. But a three-way deal also involving the Bears was voided by NFL commissioner Pete Rozelle. It was generally believed that Rozelle didn't want Davis (who had successfully sued the NFL and collected millions) to have Elway, so he blocked the deal.

And that's when the Broncos entered the fray.

The Broncos had a new owner, Edgar Kaiser Jr., grandson of American industrialist Henry J. Kaiser (Kaiser Aluminum, cars, steel, shipbuilding… everything including kitchen sinks). As the corporation had suffered hard times and Edgar, who lived in Canada, took over, he diversified. Edgar loved football. When the Phipps Bros. wanted to sell the Broncos, Rozelle put them together with Kaiser. In 1981 he paid $33 million for a franchise the Phipps' had purchased for less than $1 million. In 1984 Kaiser would double his investment when he sold the franchise to Pat Bowlen.

Owners in the league accepted Kaiser more than they had Irsay, who was belittled as "an air-conditioning salesman." Irsay had owned a very profitable (tens of millions in annual earnings) national heating and ventilation system company before he bought the Colts.

Kaiser told me much later he had befriended the Colts owner, calling him "Mr. Irsay" instead of Bob and inviting him to dinner and drinks. "I didn't have any friends in the league, either," Kaiser said, "so we sort of stuck together to ourselves."

During the Elway mess, Kaiser - who Broncos coach Red Miller said of privately "didn't know whether a football was stuffed or pumped up" -telephoned Irsay and said, "Mr. Irsay, if you decide to trade Elway, I'd be interested in doing it."

When the Raiders' trade was rejected by Rozelle, Irsay reached out to Kaiser.

Kaiser went in to see Dan Reeves, who he had hired as coach (on the recommendation of Fran Tarkenton, the ex-quarterback Kaiser had become friends with), and said, "Dan, would you like to have John Elway?"

Reeves told me later he was reminded of the conversation we'd had.

"Hell, yes. What's it gonna cost us – all our draft choices for the next year, and all arms and legs?" In fact, the Broncos offered one arm – belonging to backup quarterback Mark Herrmann, their first-round player, offensive tackle Chris Hinton, and a No. 1 pick in the 1984 draft. It didn't come out at the time, but Kaiser told me that Irsay also demanded that the Broncos play the Colts twice in exhibition games in Baltimore (guaranteeing that Elway would HAVE to play there).

The deal was consummated on May 2, 1983. I got a call from two sources (Kaiser, and shortly afterward, his secretary) that the deal was being made that day, and I put out the scoop on my afternoon radio talk show.

Years later, it was Irsay's son, Jim, who would make it possible for the Broncos to get Peyton Manning. There should be a statue to honor the Irsay father and son outside the stadium in Denver.

"I couldn't believe we pulled this off," Kaiser told me. The man who looked like 1950s TV star 'Mr. Peepers' with his wispy frame and eyeglasses, had pulled off something nobody else in football would do before or since – the most lopsided trade ever. (The Herschel Walker deal between the Vikings and the Cowboys would be a close second.)

Kaiser, though, would only be around Elway for a year before selling the team. He didn't care that much for football or Denver, honestly, and his companies were bleeding. Kaiser knew he had a cash cow in the Broncos and sold the franchise to keep his other business alive. Occasionally Kaiser would return to Denver to sit in Bowlen's box at games and we would have dinner at The Palm in downtown Denver. He wrote and sung on a CD he produced (he sounded somewhat like John Denver), owned the largest coal producing company in Canada, became a philanthropist and set a round-the-world speed record for a small plane. "I have invented a vending machine that sells French fries," he announced to me not long after he made the Elway trade. That invention was a failure. The trade was not.

Kaiser died at 69 in January, 2012, just days after the Broncos - with Elway and Manning united - lost in the playoffs to Baltimore.

Strange, wouldn't you say?

Elway's beginning in Denver was rather weird.

Reeves announced publicly, "He's going to have to beat out Steve DeBerg."

When I told Elway what Reeves said, he just laughed and laughed. Reeves and Elway got off to a turbulent start, and the relationship never really improved.

DeBerg was a journeyman NFL quarterback who had come to Denver the year before.

Elway did beat him out - for a time. He started the opening game at Pittsburgh and lined up on one play behind his left guard. After completing only one of his eight passes, he left with a minor leg injury. With DeBerg in, the Broncos would win.

The next Sunday, Elway played the entire game and won in, of all places, Baltimore, 17-10, in front of Bob Irsay. But the Broncos lost their next three, and DeBerg was promoted. Elway returned as starting quarterback in the 10th game, and the Broncos made the playoffs. Reeves started DeBerg in that game in Seattle but Elway replaced him. The Broncos lost 31-7.

Elway hated his season and, after others questioned his ability, Elway began to question himself. Many years later he would say, "It wasn't fun. I didn't like playing for Dan, and I didn't like the way I was playing." He wanted out.

The first training camp had affected Elway. The newspaper war in Denver between *Rocky Mountain News* (which, long after, ultimately died) and *The Denver Post* used Elway as their battlefield. "The Elway Watch" daily was the most popular item on every TV news show, radio talk show and newspaper front page. If he scratched his nose, or his ass, it was "news." If he threw an interception in a scrimmage, it was "big news." If Elway said he was feeling a twinge in his knee (which had been damaged badly in high school), it was "worldwide news."

One night during camp, Elway, Keith Bishop (his left guard, aka bodyguard), and I went to a local bar in Greeley, Colorado, site of the Broncos' summer training, where it was 10-beers-for-a-dollar night. We shared about $3 worth of beers. Go figure. The barflies descended on Elway. "I feel trapped," the kid said. "I can't go anywhere except my dorm room."

Life of a rock star.

I asked him how the adjustment to the NFL was going. "I know how to play this game, but Reeves, I think, wants to stifle me."

The other players loved Elway then, and from then on. Not only would he become one of the greatest players in NFL history, but he had a tough, middle-linebacker attitude and an incredible leadership quality.

In an anonymous column titled "Pike's Peek" that ran regularly in The Denver *Post*, Elway was called "Biff Elwood" because he was like an All-American kid, the super hero.

Gary Kubiak, a sixth-round draft pick out of Texas A&M, also was a quarterback. He knew, though, he would never beat out Elway and Kubiak spent the rest of his career playing rarely and learning to become a coach – which he did, as an assistant with the 49ers, an offensive coordinator under Mike Shanahan with the Broncos and, eventually, as a head coach with the Houston Texans, before being fired like most head coaches (about the same time as his former boss, Shanahan). "John's a down-to-earth guy," Kubiak told me their rookie season. The two roomed together.

Kubiak started calling Elway "Elwood" after the name in the newspaper, then "Woody." That nickname stuck on the team more than "Duke," and Elway and I would laugh about it. To have the same name as me was not his goal. When Tim Schmidt, a prominent restaurant owner in Denver, decided he wanted to open a steakhouse, he approached Elway. Brett Favre and Don Shula had their name on expensive restaurants. Why not Elway? "I told John I was thinking of calling it 'The Two Woodys' after you and him. He didn't like that. I told him I was kidding," said Schmidt, who had become one of Elway's close friends and golf partners in Denver.

"John Elway's" has become Denver's top steakhouse. Three others have been opened. Elway also would get into the car business – and co-owned a couple of dozen dealerships before eventually selling out, after his football career ended, to AutoNation for $82.5 million.

At one time, Elway was the highest-paid player in the NFL at $5 million a year.

Ha! Backups get that kind of money now.

But he made a fortune in business. Not bad for an accounting major from Stanford.

Elway and I always got along, even when I wrote negative columns about him. "You wrote good things about me and bad things, but you've always been fair to me," he said when he retired.

I've always liked Duke Elwood. He became the most famous man in Colorado, bought homes in southern California and Idaho, divorced his wife and remarried a former Oakland Raiders cheerleader, helped raise five kids (including a son who went to Arizona State to play quarterback but quit the game shortly after). John never got into trouble off the field. He treated people with respect, and he was a success in football and out of football.

I've covered thousands of athletes. I would put him at the top with Julius Erving, Dr. J, Michael Jordan, and Todd Helton. All class acts. John always looked me in the eye and told me the truth as he knew it. He is a man's man, and an athlete's athlete. There are lines in his face now, and the blond hair has touches of gray, and his gait is wobbly because of knee issues, but he is still a king, just like Elvis (who I had known and been around a long time ago and far away).

No teammate ever uttered a discouraging word about Elway. No employee of the Broncos will now that he has returned. "He brought back the same sort of culture as an executive that he brought here as a player," said a long-time executive of the Broncos. "He's John."

I've been lucky enough to be around Doak Walker, the greatest player of his era in college and pro football, and Whizzer White, still the greatest college player in the history of Colorado, and, of course, a United States Supreme Court Justice, and those three men did themselves and their sport proud. Who says anything bad about Whizzer, Doak, and The Duke? Nobody.

Yet, in his first year in Denver, John hid his misery well. He wasn't in a letter jacket anymore, and he thought he was a strange man in a strange land, especially when Reeves, to prove a point and make his stand, started DeBerg in the playoff game in Seattle, then threw Elway in after it was too late.

The Seahawks and the Broncos wouldn't meet again in the postseason for 30 years, with the same winner.

In the off-season after his rookie year, Jack Elway persuaded his son to keep playing. Good thing.

In 1984 the Broncos won 13, including their final game of the regular season in Seattle, but lost in the first round of the playoffs. Elway wouldn't ever consider quitting again, but he still didn't like Reeves. He felt the conservative coach, who had played and coached under Tom Landry in Dallas, always wanted to keep the game close, then turn Elway loose in the fourth quarter. That allowed Elway eventually to lead the league in comebacks, but didn't allow Elway to be the throwing quarterback he wanted to be.

Despite an 11-5 record in '85 (and a victory in the finale against the Seahawks, who then were members of the AFC West), the Broncos didn't make the playoffs. Elway blamed Reeves privately; Reeves blamed Elway publicly. I blamed Reeves in columns.

Denver Nuggets coach Doug Moe, who had become a good friend to Reeves, arranged for me to meet them at the Marriott restaurant in southeast Denver. That night Reeves told me, "John doesn't work hard to be a great quarterback. He refuses to learn to read defenses. We have to guess on the sideline what defense will be used and base the next play on that. He needs to be coddled."

Elway told me he wanted out of Denver. Between Reeves' offense philosophy and the *Rocky Mountain News* writing what kind of Halloween candy Elway gave out, the quarterback was frustrated.

But he was a great talent; he married his college sweetheart Janet; they bought a large home southeast of the city; John and his offensive linemen would get in the back of a pickup truck and go to wide-open land and drink beer and shoot shotguns. And Elway determined he would just outlast Reeves.

The two would never be close. Years later I wrote that Reeves should let Elway call his own plays. So Reeves let Elway call his own plays in an exhibition at San Francisco. The Broncos were pitiful offensively and afterward Reeves called me aside and said, "Satisfied now? He can't call his own plays and you don't know what you're talking about."

Yet Elway and Reeves, two hard-headed men, would go to the Super Bowl in 1986 after losing only three regular-season games, and winning in the postseason against New England and Cleveland.

The Broncos weren't as fortunate against the New York Giants during the Super Bowl. John had returned to California and got to play in the Rose Bowl (which he never reached while at Stanford). Despite having the lead at halftime, the Broncos were blown out in the second half. "We should have won that one," Elway said, and genuinely believed.

Elway and the Broncos replied with a 10-4-1 record in 1987, and again advanced to the Super Bowl (beating Cleveland again, this time in Denver), but were blown out again, this time by Washington, 42-10. They dropped to 6-8 in 1988, came back to go 11-5 in 1989 and went to the Super Bowl again. They were blown out once more, 55-10, by the San Francisco 49ers and Joe Montana. "We didn't play well, and that was the best team I ever played against," Elway says.

After the Broncos managed only a 5-11 season in 1990, Reeves, in the summer of 1991, wanted to trade Elway. Reeves had a brief conversation with Washington coach Joe Gibbs discussing a swap of Elway and quarterback Mark Rypien, who was threatening to hold out if he didn't get a new contract from Washington. But Bowlen stopped that potential blowup quickly. Bowlen never trusted Reeves again. Elway again felt he should get out of Denver and away from Reeves.

But outwardly, everything was cupcakes and moonbeams when the Broncos compiled a 12-4 record and got to the AFC Championship in 1991. They lost, though, in Buffalo after four missed field goals, an Elway interception and an Elway injury. "I got hit in the thigh, and it kept tightening up worse, until I couldn't go back in," Elway told me. Elway's career caddie, backup Gary Kubiak came in "and almost led us to victory," Elway said. "He completed every pass he threw, but we couldn't score again."

In 1992, the Broncos would finish 8-8, and Bowlen called in Elway and told the quarterback he was planning to fire Reeves and hire Mike Shanahan, who had been an assistant on and off again, under Reeves. Originally, a young Shanahan was chosen by Reeves to work with Elway. Then Shanahan became the Raiders coach. Shortly into his second season Davis fired Shanahan, and Bowlen forced Reeves to hire him back.

Reeves believed that Elway and Shanahan were plotting behind his back – scripting plays for early in the game and changing game plans from what Reeves wanted – so Reeves fired Shanahan, who went on to serve as the offensive coordinator with San Francisco, and help coach the 49ers and quarterback Steve Young to a Super Bowl victory. Shanahan told me in private two nights before the game that his objective was to score more points against the Chargers than the Broncos had given up to the 49ers in that earlier Super Bowl; he came up six short of 55 points.

After Reeves was dumped, Shanahan declined to take the job. He wanted to stay with the 49ers longer, and he didn't want to be the guy who replaced Reeves in Denver.

Instead, Bowlen promoted likeable Wade Phillips, a quality defensive coordinator, to the job. Phillips hired Jim Fassel, who had been Elway's offensive coordinator at Stanford, to join the Broncos and let John turn it loose, finally. He did. Elway had his most productive offensive season in 1993. But they lost to the Raiders in a playoff game in the Los Angeles Coliseum, where Elway never had much success. The next season the Broncos were 7-9, and Bowlen fired Phillips.

Shanahan was ready to return.

The Broncos were 8-8 in 1995, but won their first 12 games in '96 and finished 13-3.

Then they were upset by the upstart Jacksonville Jaguars in a home playoff game. Elway would call it "the most devastating loss of my career."

The next season was the Broncos' best of all time. With Terrell Davis supplying the run game to Elway's pass game, the Broncos finished 12-4, but behind Kansas City. Yet, in the playoffs, they got revenge against the Jaguars (42-10), won in Kansas City and beat the Steelers when Elway hooked up with future Hall of Fame tight end Shannon Sharpe on a key pass play in the fourth quarter.

"We had third and eight and I called a play, and Shannon said in the huddle it wasn't in the game plan," Elway told me recently. "I don't think he knew the route. I said 'Just go down past the first-down marker, and get open.'"

Sharpe told me at the Super Bowl this year, "We hadn't run the play John called since preseason. I knew the route was for six yards, and we needed eight. I told John, and he told me to shut up and go eight yards. So I did."

The pass was a success, and the Broncos would go on to score and win by three in the AFC Championship at Pittsburgh. This would be Elway's fourth Super Bowl – this time, against Green Bay and Brett Favre.

"My mother told me she didn't want me to go to the Super Bowl because she didn't want me to lose again. She was being protective," John told me.

The Broncos would win, though, with Elway pulling off one of the greatest Super Bowl moves in history.

On the 11th play of a drive, with the Broncos at the Packers 12-yard line, on third and six, the 37-year-old Elway dropped back, felt pressure and took off. Later, he and Shanahan acknowledged it was a designed play. Shanahan chose to risk Elway's body. Elway went right and knowing he had to get to the five-yard line, dove through the air, was sandwiched by two Packers and spun around, landing inside the five. The Broncos had a first down and would score to tie the game.

That play was named "The Helicopter," which would become part of the lore of Elway in the NFL.

Terrell Davis, who returned from a bad migraine to rush for three touchdowns (including a laydown on the third by the Packers, who wanted the ball back for a chance to score a tying touchdown) and 157 yards, was named MVP, but Elway got the trophy. "This one's for John," Bowlen said.

John returned for another year, another Super Bowl and another victory – this time, particularly sweet, because it was against Reeves, the Atlanta Falcons coach – and was named MVP in his final game. What a way to go out – on top back-to-back.

Five years later he was in the Hall of Fame. "Gentlemen, John Elway."

But he wasn't through with helping the Broncos get to the Super Bowl.

Elway had another comeback in him – as the leader of the Broncos.

8: AE: After Elway
MIKE KLIS

These were the Quarterback Missing Years.

It's true that when it comes to carry-the-franchise quarter-backs, the Broncos have been considerably luckier than most NFL markets. Do you think the Cleveland Browns, Kansas City Chiefs or Detroit Lions would have taken John Elway for most of the 1980s and '90s and Peyton Manning for 2012 and on into 2014?

But even Denver went through a 14-year purgatory between Elway's retirement following the 1998 season and Elway's recruit-ment of Manning in 2012.

The Broncos' quarterbacks in those 14 years all had their mo-ments. Brian Griese and Jay Cutler had Pro Bowl seasons. Jake Plummer became the winningest quarterback, in terms of winning percentage, in franchise history.

But all suffered in comparison to Elway. Broncomaniacs were spoiled. The quarterbacks A.E. could not satisfy them.

Actually, there was one more quarterback. Bubby Brister, a popu-lar veteran among Broncos teammates after he helped the team win five games during their successful Super Bowl defense in 1998, en-tered the preseason of 1999 as the No. 1 quarterback.

Four exhibition games later, Brister had played himself out of the job. Mike Shanahan made the unpopular – and perhaps wrongful – decision to switch from Brister to Griese prior to the 1999 season opener. Shanahan even admitted several years later it was the one coaching decision he'd like to have back.

But with the erratic way Brister performed during the offseason, what was the Broncos' coach supposed to do?

Brister threw three interceptions and zero touchdown passes in four preseason games, compiling a 53.9 passer rating. Griese threw six touchdown passes, one interception and had a rating of 106.5.

Still, Brister had considerable experience as an NFL starter, even if not all of it was pleasant, while Griese was entrusted to lead the two-time Super Bowl champions despite having just three pass attempts and minus-2 yards in total offense on his regular-season resume.

While the Broncos' fan base seemed mixed on the quarterback controversy, the veterans who controlled the locker room over-whelmingly wanted Bubby. The Griese era was doomed from the start.

"There was a lot of negativity" in Denver back then, Griese said during Super Bowl XLI, where he was the backup quarterback to the Chicago Bears' Rex Grossman. "I didn't necessarily know the best way to handle pressure. I became a shell of a person because I was constantly viewed as something. I learned that I am who I am and I'm comfortable with who I am."

After 16 years of Elway's rambunctious, strong-arm style that pro-duced five Super Bowl appearances and two Lombardi trophies, Broncos fans never warmed up to Griese's dunk-and-dink, game-managing style. Griese completed a high-percentage of passes and he was efficient in the 2000 season when he threw 19 touchdown passes against just 4 interceptions to earn a Pro Bowl berth even though he had missed five games with shoulder injuries.

But Griese's fate was sealed in 2002, his fourth year as the Broncos' starting quarterback, when during the offseason prior he tripped on Terrell Davis' driveway and was knocked unconscious. His bruised face and story fueled speculation Griese was falling down drunk.

And then prior to the Broncos' fourth regular-season game, a Monday nighter in Baltimore, Griese suffered a severely bruised ankle after he allegedly tripped over his dog while walking down the stairs at his home.

Worst of all, Griese lost the trust of his locker room.

"Are you jiving?" said tight end Shannon Sharpe, of the tripped-over-the-dog story. "I don't believe I'd have told that one. I'm not a very good storyteller, but I think I could have come up with a better one than that."

In March of 2003, the Broncos signed former Arizona quarterback Jake Plummer to a seven-year, $40 million contract, a move that a couple months later led to Griese's release.

Jake the Snake would have a different set of battles in Denver. A free-spirit raised in Montana and a swash-buckling star at Arizona State, Plummer was a winner on the field but often had a contentious relationship with Broncos media and fans.

He once delivered a back-of-the-head middle finger gesture to a fan heckling him during a home game at Invesco Field at Mile High. Plummer led the Broncos to three consecutive playoff berths from 2003-'05. His best season was 2005 when he cut down on his interceptions and led the Broncos to a 13-3 record and berth in the AFC championship game.

It unraveled suddenly on Plummer, though, when the Broncos lost 34–17 in the conference final against Pittsburgh. Shanahan blamed Plummer – even though Denver fell way behind in the game because its defense was torched on third-and-long conversions by Steelers' quarterback Ben Roethlisberger.

After that season, Shanahan traded up in the 2006 draft to select Vanderbilt quarterback Jay Cutler with the No. 11 pick. Plummer was on borrowed time.

In 2006, Plummer openly feuded with Shanahan on the sidelines between series. Although the Broncos were still able to begin 7-2,

Shanahan was unhappy with his offensive production. When the Broncos blew a 24-7, third quarter leader at home in their AFC West showdown with the San Diego Chargers on a Sunday night game on Nov. 19, NFL Network and former *Denver Post* reporter Adam Shefter reported Plummer would be replaced by Cutler following the team's Thanksgiving night game at Kansas City.

The pregame leak, widely believed to have been from Shanahan, was baffling because it significantly crippled the Broncos' chances of winning. Did Shanahan want to lose to Kansas City so he could further validate his decision to start Cutler?

Plummer entered the Kansas City game as a dead-quarterback walking.

"I get little bits and pieces from people," Plummer said afterwards. "People are saying, 'Hey, hang in there, don't listen to what's going on.' … The best I can, I try to shut it out because I know I have a lot of fans that are rooting hard for me. Yeah, there are some that don't want me to play anymore, but I can't control their thoughts unless I play well."

He battled, and played well at times but the Broncos lost to the Chiefs, 19-10.

Even though Plummer posted an impressive 39-15 record in his 3 ½ seasons with the Broncos, Thanksgiving night in Kansas City would mark the final start of his career.

Cutler took over but only went 2-3 in the final five games – including a pick six in final-game loss against 6-9 San Francisco where a win would have put the Broncos in the playoffs for a fourth consecutive year.

Instead, the Broncos began a skid of five consecutive years without a playoff appearance.

While with the Bears, Griese paid close attention to the quarterback switch in Denver.

"I know how Jake feels, and it's a tough spot," Griese said. "It wasn't all Jake's fault. And it never is. But the first one to go is the quarterback."

Griese's advice for Cutler as his Denver days were taking off? "Be yourself. ... The city is demanding."

After the season, Plummer let it be known he would retire, but because the quarterback owed the team a $5 million payback on his signing bonus if he did quit, Shanahan stuck it to him and traded him to Tampa Bay.

Plummer kept to his word and retired at 32, even though he did later have to write a $5 million check to the Bucs. Ouch.

The 2007 season began with Plummer retired to the Sawtooth Mountains in Idaho and Cutler as the Broncos' new franchise quarterback.

"I don't want to take anything away from Jake Plummer, because he won 70 percent of our games and he did a lot of great things when he was here," Shanahan said. "But it's a new era, and we have a quarterback with different skills."

Cutler started 2-0 in 2007 thanks to an enervating, last-tick, fire-drill field goal by Jason Elam to stun Buffalo in the opener, and Shanahan calling a timeout just before Raiders' kicker Sebastian Janikowski booted what would have been a 52-yard, game-winning field goal in overtime. After celebrating his field goal that didn't count, Janikowski pelted the ball of the right upright with his next kick and the Broncos went on for a game-winning field goal drive.

But after that promising start – Shanahan's teams always started well and faded badly – the Broncos lost nine of their next 13 games. Cutler dropped weight as the season went along.

And then came an example as to why the media and the subjects they cover can never form personal friendships. As the Broncos' beat reporter, I received a tip that Cutler was diagnosed with Type 1 diabetes on May 1, 2008. According to the tipster, the players already knew.

I got Cutler's condition confirmed by two other sources, including Jay's father, Jack. In the two years since the Broncos drafted Cutler, I had talked frequently with his father, mostly on the phone. Jack let me know I was not to report on Cutler's diabetes or we would never speak again.

I told him I had no choice because it possibly could have had impact on his son's past and future performance as the Broncos' quarterback. I also tried to tell Jack that by reporting the diabetes, Jay would receive not criticism but sympathy and understanding.

Jack insisted I not report it. I felt I had to report it. As I was writing the story, I received a text from Jay saying I should delete his number and that we would never speak again. I broke the story, portraying Cutler in a positive, even courageous manner, but no matter. The Cutlers didn't talk to me the rest of the 2008 season.

And I didn't blame them. I understood. A medical condition is private. But Jay Cutler is a public figure. I believed I did the right thing as a journalist. And the Cutlers had the right to be upset.

Jack Cutler was nothing but protective of his son. His ill-feelings toward me, after the numerous conversations on all things football and non-football subjects, were understandable.

By way of Broncos media relations director Patrick Smyth, Jay Cutler and I had a peace treaty lunch in January, 2009, at a poolside table in Hawaii. Cutler had a sensational start to the 2008 season, throwing for 8 touchdowns and 914 yards while leading the Broncos to a 3-0 record and 38.0 points per game.

But like in 2007, the 2008 season unraveled on the Broncos, first by losing four of their next five, then losing their final three games to become the first team in NFL history to have a three-game lead with three to play and not make the playoffs.

Still, Cutler's season was terrific overall and still stands today as his best. He threw for 25 touchdowns and more than 4,500 yards. He also threw 18 interceptions – way too many in today's short-passing, high-percentage era – but he made the Pro Bowl and he was only 25.

Two days after the season ended with an embarrassing, 52-21, playoff-eliminating loss at San Diego, the Broncos fired Shanahan. Not two weeks later, the Broncos would replace Shanahan with Josh McDaniels.

Suddenly, shockingly, the Cutler era in Denver would soon be finished, too.

9: The McMess

MIKE KLIS

Jay Cutler was fresh off a Pro Bowl but filled with sore feelings as he sat in the office of his cocksure, baby-faced head coach.

Cutler, the Broncos' young, gun-slinging quarterback, and Josh McDaniels, the team's recently hired successor of the once iconic Mike Shanahan, were not unlike petulant teenage jocks from the same high school who liked the same girl.

Their meeting was supposed to be a peace treaty. Instead, Cutler walked out disgusted and certain he would not spend one more day referring to McDaniels as his coach.

Thus began the stormy, brief, Captain Queeg-like leadership tenure of Josh McDaniels. He grew up in Canton, Ohio as the quarterback-playing son of a legendary high school football coach. He made his mark as the top offensive assistant to Bill Belichick, the great coach of the New England Patriots. In heavy demand as a bright, young, up-and-coming head coach, McDaniels was hired by the Broncos in January, 2009, only to be fired less than two years later after guiding the Broncos through an insufferable 5-17 stretch that followed questionable personnel moves ("With the No. 25 pick in the 2010 draft, the Denver Broncos select... Tim Tebow!"), volatile outbursts in public view on the sidelines and behind closed doors in the upstairs offices at Dove Valley, fallouts with young stars Cutler, Brandon Marshall, Tony Scheffler and Peyton Hillis, a videotape spying scandal, and an increasing disconnect with a fan base that never did warm up to this hoodie-wearing, know-it-all from the New England Way.

It was an unfortunate coaching period that began with an unimaginable fallout with his 25-year-old, strong-armed quarterback.

The meeting in McDaniels' office on March 11, 2009 was supposed to clear up a misunderstanding. Sitting next to Cutler was his agent James "Bus" Cook. Sitting alongside McDaniels was Broncos general manager Brian Xanders.

It was a meeting of unintended adversaries because Cutler learned on Feb. 28 – six weeks after McDaniels had been hired by Broncos owner Pat Bowlen to replace the then iconic Mike Shanahan – that McDaniels had contemplated trading him to Tampa Bay in a three-team deal that would have brought McDaniels' former quarterback in New England, Matt Cassel, to Denver.

Matt Cassel?

"My understanding at this point is they're trying to trade me," Cutler told *The Denver Post* on Feb. 28. "We'll see where I end up at. I liked it here, I liked playing with these guys, but obviously they're not going to let me have that opportunity."

To be fair to McDaniels, he briefly entertained the thought of dealing with Cutler in part because he knew Cutler had twice issued trade demands – the first after the Broncos fired Shanahan, and the second after McDaniels' hiring meant a certain end for offensive co-ordinator Jeremy Bates.

And indeed, Bates – who, like McDaniels, was a 32-year-old offensive dynamo – was dismissed. Cutler had eventually settled down, though, and came around to thinking working with McDaniels might not be so bad. After all, McDaniels was Tom Brady's offensive coordinator in New England, where in 2007 he helped the Patriots score a record 589 points – 36.8 per game – while going 16-0 in the regular season.

"What bothers me about this is I've been dropping in there regularly the last 2 1/2 weeks, dealing with these guys, talking to Mr. Bowlen, talking to Josh, talking to (offensive coordinator) Mike McCoy," Cutler said, "day to day... and they didn't reach this point yesterday, you know what I mean? It's been in motion for a while."

McDaniels downplayed the seriousness of a Cutler-Cassel swap, saying he was approached with the proposal but never gave it enough consideration to where he brought it to the owner's attention.

Cassel was instead traded to the Kansas City Chiefs on Feb. 28, but Cutler was nevertheless shaken by reports his team entertained moving him.

"I'm upset. I mean I'm really shocked at this point," he said. "I could see why they want Cassel. I don't know if they think I can't run the system or I don't have the skills for it. I just don't get it. Or if they don't think they can sign me with my next contract. I just don't know what it is. I've heard I'm still on the trading block."

Twelve days later, Cutler was in McDaniels' office. The moment of truth came when Cutler threw it up to the coach. "Can you at least tell me you won't trade me?"

McDaniels, who at 32 was woefully inexperienced at dealing with people outside an offensive film room, handled a sensitive situation with the delicacy of a middle linebacker ramming forward on a fourth-and-1.

He bluntly told Cutler that all players could be traded. He said it in a way that Cutler took as confrontational. Cutler got up and left.

The next day, Cook formally issued a trade request to the Broncos at his client's request.

"I went in there with every intention of solving the issue, being a Bronco, moving forward as a Bronco," Cutler told ESPN.com about the meeting. "We weren't in there but about 20 minutes, (McDaniels) did most of the talking, and as far as I'm concerned, he made it clear he wants his own guy. He admitted he wanted Matt Cassel because he said he has raised him up from the ground as a quarterback. He said he wasn't sorry about it.

"At the end of the meeting, he wasn't like, 'Jay, I want you as our quarterback, you're our guy.' It felt like the opposite... Really, I figured we'd hash things out, shake hands, laugh a little and move forward. What happened (Saturday) was the last thing I expected."

Bowlen attempted to contact Cutler but the quarterback refused to either take the owner's call, or call him back.

"I'm very disappointed," Bowlen said. "I'm disappointed in the whole picture, not just disappointed that we might lose our star quarterback."

A frustrated Bowlen gave McDaniels the order to trade away his insubordinate quarterback.

The divorce was officially filed on April 2, when Cutler and a fifth-round draft pick were dealt to the Bears for quarterback Kyle Orton, two first-round draft picks and a third-round selection.

It was Monday night, Dec. 6, 2010 and Bowlen, accompanied by his wife Annabel, was having dinner with John Elway and his wife Paige. The dinner was at Elway's Steakhouse in downtown Denver.

The significance of the dinner double-date? A few hours earlier, Bowlen had called Josh McDaniels into his office and dismissed the worst mistake he had made in his 27 years as the Broncos' owner.

It was no coincidence McDaniels was fired a little more than a week after it was revealed the team was caught in a videotape violation.

Although Bowlen and Ellis, along with an NFL investigative team, determined McDaniels was unaware that Broncos video coordinator Steve Scarnecchia broke a coveted "integrity-of-the-game" policy by taping a six-minute portion of the San Francisco 49ers' walkthrough practice on Oct. 30 in London, the coach's failure to report the incident was deemed unforgivable among upper management.

The Denver Post broke the story, after which the NFL moved quickly to announce $50,000 fines against McDaniels, and the team, the same day. Broncos' management has not said who reported the violation to them, which they investigated before informing the NFL.

Bowlen and Elway have always said their dinner that night was a coincidence. Elway said the date was scheduled well before Bowlen had decided to fire McDaniels.

Yet a month later, Bowlen hired Elway to take over the Broncos' football operations department.

In a perverse sense, the Broncos would not be where they are today as AFC champions had the McMess never happened. If not for McDaniels, the Broncos would have had no reason to bring in Elway to raise the sinking ship. If not for McDaniels, the Broncos would have never hired John Fox to become head coach.

All Elway and Fox did as the head of the Broncos' football management team was lead Denver to three AFC West Division titles in three years.

Had it not been for McDaniels, the Broncos' quarterback would have still been Jay Cutler, now 31 and still with the Chicago Bears but with only one playoff appearance – and zero Super Bowl berths – in his eight NFL seasons.

Then again, if not for McDaniels, the Broncos and their fan base would have been deprived of the Magic of Tebow. Even if it was short-lived, Tebow's 2011 season will go down as one of the most intoxicating phenomena to ever descend upon the NFL.

It was McDaniels, too, who drafted the likes of running back Knowshon Moreno, defensive end Robert Ayers, receivers Demaryius Thomas and Eric Decker, guard Zane Beadles and special teams standout David Bruton – all major contributors to the Broncos' reaching the Super Bowl in 2013.

Narrowed strictly to his coaching tenure, McDaniels was a disaster, a poor leader of men. But there was some brilliance laced among the McMadness. To get to where they are now, the Broncos first had to go through the Josh McDaniels experience.

10: Tebowmania, For Overtime and a Short Time
WOODY PAIGE

Whatever happened to Tim Tebow?

For over seven years, during his four seasons at the University of Florida and three seasons with the Denver Broncos and the New York Jets, Tebow was one of the most celebrated, popular, despised, loved, loathed, mocked, bizarre, idolized quarterbacks... no, make that athletes... no, make that famous people, in the world.

The sports website Deadspin.com once counted that commentators and anchors had said the name "Tebow" 160 times in one hour.

Due to his personality, his (sarcastic) egotistical declarations, and his views on religion and war, there has not been such a polarizing figure in sports since Muhammad Ali. For Tim Tebow, it was all about his religious convictions, his beliefs, his virginity and his play, or non-play, at quarterback – and passing.

John Lennon once harked that the Beatles were more popular than Jesus, and he got the wrath of God from religious fanatics. Tim Tebow was arguably, for a time, as well-known as the Beatles had been and up there (figuratively) with Jesus Christ – who was, as

Tebow always pointed out in every post-game interview "my Lord and savior."

During a span of about three months, Tebow, in fact, was the Denver Broncos' savior.

Tebow was arguably the greatest college football player of all time. Heisman Trophy? He was the first sophomore to win it. He finished in the top three voting two other times. In 2008, he had more first-place votes than the winner, Sam Bradford. But too many voters in the southwest region left Tebow off their ballot.

Tebow's Florida Gators then routed Bradford's Oklahoma Sooners in the national championship game. Take that, Albuquerque.

It was the second national title Tebow helped win for the Gators. His first came as a special-package force in his freshman season, when he made the "jump pass" famous, and then as the unquestioned quarterback leader of the 2008 Florida Gators, when he made an even more famous "Promise."

Besides a Heisman that should have been two, and a national championship that did become two, Tebow had all the statistics to support the claim as best-ever college player. He would not only rush for nearly 3,000 yards with 57 touchdowns - unheard of totals for a quarterback - he finished with the second-highest rated passer in college history, with an efficiency of 170.8 on 88 touchdown passes against 16 interceptions.

And he delivered the most famous rah-rah speech this side of Knute Rockne's "win one for the Gipper." Tebow's motivational oratory, delivered after a 31-30 upset loss to Ole Miss, was dubbed "The Promise" and is immortalized in a plaque that hangs outside the Gators' football complex attached to The Swamp.

Tebow was the epitome of the All American boy, a handsome, wholesome, God-worshipping, ever-positive kid with nary a bad word to say about anybody.

Yet, once Tebow became a professional quarterback for the Denver Broncos, half the world couldn't stand him.

No doubt some of the love-him or hate-him conflict was because of his strong Christian beliefs. Not religious beliefs. Tebow is a non-denominational Christian. He unfailingly used his platform as a star athlete to profess his faith in Jesus Christ as the Lord, Savior and only Son of God.

Grandmas and football "widows" loved him. Christians admired him. Republican politicians and LeBron James stood behind him.

Others rolled their eyes, or even detested him, believing his popularity was magnified only because of his faith.

But the divide on Tebow wasn't just about Christianity. There was also tremendous disagreement on Tebow's ability as a quarterback.

Tebow has maintained since he was 8, "My dream is to play quarterback in the NFL."

In the years 2010, 2011 and 2012, for 17 games, he lived the dream.

After those mind-boggling four years at Florida, there were serious questions about Tebow's future in the NFL as a quarterback. Many thought he should switch to tight end or running back. But his dream was to play quarterback in the NFL.

So, Timmy, as his parents have always called him and as he refers to himself when he calls you, trained with several quarterback gurus because scouts believed his throwing motion was too scattered and started too low on his body and too far back. He had been a good baseball pitcher, and he threw a football as if it were a baseball. Zeke Bratkowski, a former Green Bay Packers quarterback, mentored Tebow for several days in Florida and told me later, "I had him throw routes blind-folded and he completed every pass. He can be a very good NFL quarterback once he learns a system. He's the most competitive player I've ever been around."

Others disagreed.

Legendary football coach Jimmy Johnson was one who opened fire on what would become a three-year verbal war against Tebow's prospects as an NFL quarterback.

"I don't think Tebow can play in a pro-style offense, not quarterback," Johnson said on the Dan Patrick radio show. "I think a team that's going to look at Tim Tebow, they're going to make one of two decisions. If they're going to bring him into their style of play, with their coaching staff, they've got to project him to be maybe an H-back.

«I don't know if he's fast enough to be a receiver, maybe he could be a tight end. I don't know if he can block, I don't know if he can catch the ball. But he's got to play another position. He can't play quarterback.»

Most NFL teams weren't interested.

The Broncos were. New coach Josh McDaniels had been the quarterbacks' coach then offensive coordinator at New England, and had been alongside Tom Brady, who was chosen in the sixth round, and coached backup Matt Cassel, who had not been a starter in college or the pros, but took over when Brady was hurt in 2008 and produced an exceptional season. McDaniels believed he could transform Tebow into a great NFL quarterback.

McDaniels and general manager Brian Xanders had flown down to Florida and put Tebow through a workout and "board" exercise where players are to diagram plays, formations, and coverages. Later, he showed me tapes of Tebow throwing. "His elbow is too wide open. It's like in golf. He's got to keep the elbow closer to his body. We showed him that change, and he was throwing it perfect. Look at the difference," McDaniels said as he paused the tape, then set it in slow-motion. "I can do great things with him. I asked him about defenses and he answered every question. He has a high QB IQ, and he can read defenses and knows offenses."

McDaniels intended to draft Tebow in the first round, and had informed Tebow's rep – Jimmy Sexton, a prominent agent based in Memphis, Tenn. Sexton and Tebow flew into Denver for another session with McDaniels and his offensive coaches, and Sexton told Tebow on the flight South he would be picked by the Broncos. For the draft, Tebow decided he'd rather be home with his family in Jacksonville than in the green room of New York's Radio City Music Hall, where the event was held. He was uncertain if he would be drafted in the first round and he didn't want to be embarrassed sitting in the green room into later rounds, as others had been before him. In Florida, Sexton bought a dozen Broncos caps (and an equal number of caps from other teams) and stashed them in a bedroom at the home of Tebow's parents, Bob and Pam, who had met when they were students at Florida.

As the first half of the first round was completed, Tim became nervous and wanted to go outside and throw a football. Brother Robby, his confidante, joined him.

When Denver's turn came up at No. 22, the family and friends and Sexton got ready to cheer in the comfortable ranch-style home, with a pool and plenty of acreage, outside Jacksonville.

But the Broncos chose wide receiver Demaryius Thomas from Georgia Tech. (McDaniels had dropped in on Thomas, who had a foot injury, on his trip back from Florida after visiting with Tebow).

Tebow was devastated. It was now feared that he wouldn't go in the first round. Patriots' coach Bill Belichick had brought Tebow in, and took him to dinner at a South Boston Italian restaurant, but New England had Brady, and didn't want to cause an issue by drafting Tebow.

Meanwhile, the Broncos were wheeling and dealing, and acquired another first round pick at No. 25. "That will be us," Sexton told Tebow.

Then McDaniels called. "Yes, sir, I'm ready and excited," Tebow said.

When McDaniels daringly selected the quarterback with the No. 25 overall pick in the 2010 draft, the NFL world – particularly the experts – wondered if the new young head coach was a loony tunes egomaniac.

And maybe he was. But Tebow was also a gift, the likes of which the Broncos and city of Denver will never come across again.

The day after he was drafted Tebow flew into Denver and said he would do whatever it took to become the Broncos' quarterback, and he was prepared to stay and get in the Broncos' weight room and on the field every day. He was informed that NFL rules prohibited drafted players from being at the team's headquarters until the first off-season minicamp. Tebow had to go home. I wrote a column that was placed prominently, with Tebow's photo, on the front page of *The Denver Post*. I suggested he could become a great quarterback because of his work ethic and athletic ability.

I had been right many years before about John Elway.

Patrick Smyth called me the day after the draft and said Tebow had left me a present, and could I come to Dove Valley?

"A present? You got to be kidding."

"He loved your column."

So, somewhat amused, I drove over to the team's offices. Patrick gave me a copy of The *Post*. "I have one of these at home," I said.

"Not like this one."

On the cover Tebow had written, "Mr. Paige, Thanks for support-ing me. I look forward to proving you right. God Bless!" And he added his signature.

Wild child.

Shortly after, McDaniels agreed to meet me in his office. I asked, "What are you going to do at quarterback?" He had veteran Kyle Orton as a returning starter, and had traded with the Browns for another former No. 1 pick and Notre Dame quarterback Brady Quinn, and here comes Tebow.

"Turn off your tape recorder," he said.

He talked for a while about Kyle Orton's lack of off-season workouts, his poor attitude, and his lack of leadership then said, "What if I told you Orton wasn't going to be here this year?"

"I wouldn't believe you."

But, then, McDaniels already had traded Jay Cutler the previous year for the Bears' Orton, and Orton had proven to be a mediocre quarterback with a strong arm.

"You just wait and see, but don't quote me about this," McDaniels said.

Orton wasn't traded, as it turned out, and twice I called out McDaniels on what he had told me. "There's a reason," he said.

When McDaniels was fired, I asked Joe Ellis about the McDaniels-Orton stuff, and said the coach had lied to me about trading Orton. "No, he didn't. He told me he wanted to trade Orton. He was going to get rid of him. But, for the only time Josh was here, I talked him out of something. I told him to at least wait and see how Tebow and Quinn turned out."

As it was, neither young player turned out to be so good. Quinn was average, at best, as has been proven time and again during his career. He never played a down with the Broncos, and was awful as a starter with the Chiefs. Now, he's destined to be a backup for as long as he stays around the league.

And Tebow was a horrendous player in practice, as he has been ever since. As he rehearsed plays, Tebow threw his passes into the turf, over the heads of receivers, into the crowds – record crowds at Dove Valley watching pre-season workouts. Allen Iverson, who would play for the Denver Nuggets late in his career, had provided one of the most famous quotes in sports history when he was All-NBA with the Philadelphia 76ers and was asked about his lackadaisical attitude at practices. "We're sitting here, and I'm supposed to be the franchise player, and we're talking about practice. I mean listen, we're sitting here talking about practice, not a game, not a game, not a game, but we're talking about practice. Not the game that I go out there and die for and play every game like it's my last but we're talking about practice man. How silly is that?"

Tebow would sort of agree with Iverson. He really wasn't about practice. You can't practice what he does best when a play breaks down. He'll take off, run through six defenders and pick up 13 yards, or throw off the wrong foot and complete a 20-yard pass in traffic. He was a guy you'd love in a pickoff game – or maybe, if he ever was inserted as a start, in a real game.

"What people don't realize about Tim is that he's what I call a lights-on player. The things he does well don't show up in practice. But when you turn the lights on in a game, that's when he turns it on," a former Florida assistant coach told me.

The Broncos' first game of the 2010 season was in, ironically, Jacksonville, his hometown, against the team everybody felt Tebow would play for in the pros. But the Jaguars had no interest, odd given that the franchise was in danger of moving because of declining attendance and attention.

McDaniels was stuck with Orton, who started the game.

Tebow rushed twice in the game in the "wildcat" offense, and managed just two yards.

In the six games that Tebow was inserted, he ran only 12 times and threw three passes. But the Broncos scored four touchdowns on those plays.

After the 12th game of the season, a loss in Kansas City, and with the Broncos staggering to 3-9 record, McDaniels was fired.

After another loss, Tebow started his first game in Oakland. The dream was realized, even if the Broncos lost, despite a good effort by Tebow, on a muddy field.

In his second start Tebow would lead the Broncos to a comeback victory at home over the Texans. He was impressive in all three starts, but lost two.

With the takeover of John Elway as executive vice president of football operations and John Fox as head coach, supposedly the No. 1 quarterback spot would be wide open among Tebow, Orton, and Quinn. But first, there was a lockout of NFL players, and no summer off-season programs or minicamps.

When the lockout finally ended, the Broncos — believe it or not — tried to trade Orton, which McDaniels had wanted to do the year before. Elway had made a deal with the Miami Dolphins, but it couldn't be completed because Orton wouldn't accept the terms of Miami's new contract offer.

And Fox, embarrassingly, made Orton his starter.

Tebow was upset, but he put on a happy face and said he would work harder to prove himself.

With Orton at quarterback, the Broncos continued to struggle and were 1-3 and trailing the San Diego Chargers in Denver, when Fox replaced Orton with Tebow.

Tebow nearly pulled off a victory when he threw and ran for two touchdowns.

The next week was a bye, and when Fox was asked who would be the starter in the next game at Miami, he suggested in his mid-week press conference that Orton would be back at quarterback. After the meeting with the media, on his way out of the room, I asked Fox if he really was doing the right thing, and he half-whispered to me that the right thing was not always the thing that you have to do. A radio guy said, "Did he say to you what I think he said and what do you think that means?"

"I think he means the right thing to do is to start Tebow, but he can't."

But here's what happened: Fox decided to do the right thing and told his offensive coaches he wanted to make a permanent change to Tebow. Offensive coordinator Mike McCoy tried to talk Fox out of the move, saying that if it had to be done, the Broncos should go with Quinn. But Fox's mind was set in concrete. "Let's see what the kid can do. Get out the plays he ran in Florida, and let's do some read-option and see what happens." The offensive coaches thought Fox was going to go down and take them with him. McCoy thought he would never get another coaching job in the NFL (he would end up as the head coach of the Chargers, partially because of the creative ways he used Tebow).

Tebow would start in Ft. Lauderdale against Miami in a game, oddly enough, that already had been designated as a reunion for the Tebow-Florida championship team.

On the way to the stadium, Mike Klis and I talked in the car about what would happen in the game. "If I were a betting man, I'd take the Dolphins," Mike said. "I'll bet you a dollar Tebow wins this. It's so big for him."

I won the bet... barely.

The Broncos were horrible and through three quarters in his first start against Miami, Tebow was worse. With 5:23 remaining in the game, Tebow was 4 of 14 for 40 yards. The Broncos were 0 of 10 on third-down conversions. The team was down 15-0 to the Dolphins with a little more than 3 minutes to go.

And then Tebow started playing like Steve Young. He engineered one touchdown drive. A recovered onside kick (it could only happen with Tebow at quarterback!) started another touchdown drive.

He threw two touchdown passes and ran in a two-point conversion to tie it. Matt Prater kicked a 52-yard field goal in overtime. Broncos win! Tebowing was born and kneel prayer upon kneel prayer swept the country.

After a miserable, low-down, no-good performance the following week, a 45-10 loss at home to the Detroit Lions, Fox and offensive coordinator Mike McCoy installed a college-type, read-option offense – and pulled out tapes of Tebow's plays in college. With the new, "unusual" offense, the Broncos whipped the stunned Oakland Raiders, 38-24. Tebow threw for two touchdowns and ran for 118 yards. It was the Florida Gators all over again.

The next week he was just 2 of 8 passing against Kansas City. But one completion was a 57-yard touchdown to Eric Decker and Tebow ran for another score.

Down 13-10 late on a Thursday night against the New York Jets, Tebow capped a 95-yard drive with a 20-yard scrambling touchdown run with 58 seconds left. Tebow did it again.

The Broncos were trailing in the fourth quarter of their next three games. Tebow came through in each to beat San Diego in overtime, Minnesota with 0:00 left in regulation and the Chicago Bears in overtime.

People across the country were "Tebowing" – defined as kneeling in prayer, even if everyone around you is doing something completely different.

The harshest of Tebow's critics were apologizing. No one was more severe than former running back Merrill Hoge, an ESPN analyst who tweeted out in August, "It's embarrassing to think the Broncos could win with Tebow!"

In December, Hoge delivered a mea culpa on the Mike & Mike radio show.

"I've been obviously very hard on Tim Tebow, very critical of him as a quarterback and his skill set," Hoge said. "I've been wrong on a lot of levels with him. I've lost the ability, or the opportunity, I should say to shed light on what an amazing story, how he has worked, persevered, changed – his diligence – all those things that you try to teach young people – what sports are really about."

Just as everyone was jumping on the Tebow bandwagon, the wheels started to fall off. The Broncos lost their final three games of the season. Tebow played poorly in the last two, against lowly Buffalo and Kansas City.

Heading into the playoff game against the heavily favored Steelers, Fox not-so-discreetly implied he would pull Tebow for backup quarterback Brady Quinn at halftime if Tebow played like he did in the previous two games.

Tebow rose to the challenge. He completed passes of 51 and 58 yards to Thomas. He threw a 30-yard touchdown pass to Eddie Royal and ran in for another score in a 20-point second quarter to put the Broncos up by two touchdowns.

The Steelers, though, would rally. It was 23-23 at the end of regulation. The Broncos won the flip and took the ball.

Several days earlier, I had interviewed John Elway about his first year as head of Broncos football operations. At the end of the telephone interview, I asked Elway, "Are you going to talk to Tebow before the game (with Pittsburgh)?"

"Nah, I don't want to mess with his head."

"Well, what would you say to him if you did talk to him?"

"Pull the trigger."

Like everyone else, Elway knew that Tebow was too hesitant, too late with his throws, too quick to run when a play broke down.

I put down the phone and said loudly, "I just got the money shot."

The lead paragraph in my story the next day was that Elway wanted Tebow to "pull the trigger."

It became the biggest story in the country. Not sports story. Story. Here was the Hall of Fame quarterback ordering his young quarterback to throw the damn football. Naturally, Tebow was asked the next day about his reaction to the Elway quote.

"He's right," Tebow said.

Elway had gotten his message to Tebow, through me.

In the four quarters Tebow threw 20 times and completed nine for 236 yards and a touchdown, without an interception. The Broncos scored 23 points. The Steelers, behind Ben Roethlisberger, rallied for 10 points in the last 10 minutes to send the game into overtime tied at 23.

In the foreword of this book, Jim Nantz, the No. 1 play-by-play announcer for CBS, describes what had happened when he talked to the coaches the night before about a possible overtime.

The Broncos got the ball. On the first play, Mundy had shifted from his deep safety position up closer to the line of scrimmage. Cornerback Ike Taylor kept creeping toward the line. The Steelers now had all 11 defenders in the box area, a strategic maneuver by defensive coordinator Dick LeBeau that dared Tebow to throw.

In a long list of miracles, Tebow had one more in him. He took the shotgun snap from J.D. Walton, cocked his left arm behind his head, and threw a perfect completion 15 yards downfield to receiver Demaryius Thomas, who was running a simple crossing pattern from left to right.

All Thomas had to do was beat cornerback Ike Taylor off the line. He did. After catching the Tebow pass, Thomas delivered a deadly stiff-arm to Taylor, knocking the corner out of the play. Thomas was off and running.

Mundy scrambled to recover and at one point he had the angle on Thomas. The receiver ran away from him, then pulled a Bo Jackson and ran straight into the tunnel that led to the victorious locker room.

"I was coming back out, and I got crushed," Thomas said of his celebrating teammates. "Everybody got me in the tunnel."

Tebow ran down the field screaming, yelling, thanking the Lord. He had passed for John 3:16 – 316 yards – and he kept running until he reached the South Stands, whereupon he jumped in. Tim Tebow's last play in Denver was his first Mile High leap. The cameras missed it.

The sellout crowd of 75,970 at Sports Authority Field at Mile High erupted in celebration. Witnesses said that in Denver neighborhoods, delirious people were screaming from their balconies. Patrons at Denver-area bars were heard chanting, "Te-bow! Te-bow!" Tebowmania was once again inflated.

In the second playoff game in New England (the Patriots had beaten Tebow and the Broncos in Denver in the 14th regular-season game), Tebow would suffer a severely bruised sternum, but the injury didn't matter. The Patriots overwhelmed him and the Broncos. It was a blowout and a blow to Tebow.

Nevertheless, after the season, Elway said publicly that Tebow would be the starter heading into the 2012 camp.

But John wasn't convinced. "I think he's a great athlete and competitor," John told me one day in his office. "We just have to find out if he can be a great quarterback."

Elway intended to draft a college quarterback and get him ready to take over at some juncture if Tebow, and Tebowing, didn't succeed. There was also discussion about the Broncos obtaining another veteran quarterback just in case…

The Broncos did get a veteran QB: Peyton Manning, who had been released by the Indianapolis Colts. But this wasn't an "in case" situation. Manning, arguably, is the greatest quarterback in NFL history, and he had chosen, as a free agent, to join the Broncos. Tebow wouldn't be the starter. He wouldn't be the backup. He wouldn't even be in Denver.

Tebow's brief, flaming career in Denver was over. Tebowmania evaporated.

He would be traded. There were offers from Jacksonville and the New York Jets. Fox persuaded Tebow and Sexton that Tim's best deal was the Jets. Fox knew that the Jaguars' coaching staff didn't want Tebow; this was a move by the Jags' new owner to bring the circus to town and sell tickets for a struggling franchise. Tebow had led a Thursday night comeback victory over the Jets the previous season, and coach Rex Ryan (who would later deny he had any interest in Tebow) and the Jets thought Tebow could do for them what he had done to them.

Tebow replaced Ringling Bros. Barnum & Bailey in New York, but not Mark Sanchez. Despite all the back-page tabloid hoopla and a ground-shaking press conference when Tebow arrived, he never really got to play for the Jets.

He was a mere sideshow.

At the end of the season he was gone. He should have taken the Jacksonville trade. Blaine Gabbert, the Jags' quarterback, would be replaced, and ultimately traded, in March of 2014, for a nothing draft choice from San Francisco. The Jaguars would have to start over. Dan Patrick said on his show one day in March, "If Tebow were in Jacksonville, he'd still be in the league, and maybe even starting the past season."

And, interestingly, Tebow ended up in 2013 with New England and Bill Belichick, who had liked him out of college, and the Patriots' offensive coordinator was, guess who, Josh McDaniels. Timmy and Josh back together.

What goes around surely does come around.

It didn't work out. Tebow played... interestingly... in the final exhibition, but was cut before the regular season and didn't play for anybody in 2013.

In the NFL Tebow compiled a 9-7 regular-season and postseason record as a starter and had thrown for 2,874 yards and 19 touchdowns and had rushed for 1,052 yards and 13 touchdowns.

Where have you gone, Timmy Tebow?

He signed a contract with ESPN to work as an analyst for the new SEC-ESPN network for the 2014 football season, and Tim appeared as a commentator on ESPN before and at halftime of the BCS Championship. He did a commercial for a cellphone company that was considered the most popular that appeared during the Super Bowl. In it, Tebow satirizes himself, talking about how you don't need a contract and all that he had done during the '13 season – helping a woman give birth in a hospital, being a comic and a rock star, racing cars, starring in an action movie, playing chess with a grandmaster, searching for and tackling Bigfoot, and speaking at the United Nations.

Tebow will never go away. He will always be on a big stage, whatever that is.

Senator Tebow?

President Tebow?

There are options and possibilities beyond football and broadcasting.

Or he could be signed by an NFL team before the 2014 season as a quarterback. Or would Tebow be willing to give up his dream to be an NFL quarterback?

As I've written, the new A11FL, a spring league, will begin play in 2015 in eight major cities. Commissioner Scott McKibben contacted Tebow's agent and his lawyer and made an offer to Tebow to join the league as a quarterback and a part owner of a franchise. "We'd love to have Tim Tebow in our league. He represents all the qualities we look for in a player," McKibben told me.

Would it be possible that Tebow returns to Denver and plays quarterback for the A11FL?

League people have reached out to Tebow's people, but there have been no comments from Tebow. Although he has been hired by ESPN as an analyst on the new SEC network, Tebow still wants to play in the NFL and has an out-clause. A spring league wouldn't interfere with his fall job on TV, and the A11FL hopes Tebow will be the face of the league and play in its kickoff games this spring for Tampa Bay. ESPN will televise both games and a game-of-the-week in '15.

If Denver, as expected, gets a franchise, Tebow would look fashionable in a blue No. 15 jersey. His, uh, resurrection in Denver will bring out the multitude of Tebowlicious fanatics and the detractor trailers.

It would be fun.

W.W.T.D.? What will Timmy do?

11: Peyton Manning: A New Sheriff In Dusty Old Cowtown

MIKE KLIS

Blame Peyton Manning on Broncos president Joe Ellis.

It was shortly after the Broncos lost their 2011 regular-season finale to Kansas City, 7-3. Tim Tebow was 6 of 22 for 60 yards in that game. That followed a three-interception, 40-14, Christmas Eve disaster in Buffalo.

Tebowmania was no longer a slow leak but a Katrina-sized breach.

Ellis walked out of his office, made a left down the carpeted hallway and walked into the office of John Elway.

"What do you think the chances are of us winding up with Peyton Manning?" Ellis said.

Elway was a slightly taken aback. He had only been the Broncos executive vice president of football operations for a little more than a year, but that was long enough for him to believe it would be a struggle for the team to come up with the money to sign such a prize.

"We'll find the money," Ellis said.

The seeds of Peyton Manning playing for the Broncos had been planted.

Manning had not played in 2011 because of his neck issue and as his Indianapolis Colts slid to 2-14 and the No. 1 draft pick without him, it became apparent one of the league's all-time best quarterbacks would soon be made available to the free-agent market.

Give Tebow credit for lifting the franchise back to a level of respectability where Manning could not immediately dismiss the Broncos' advances outright.

"Tim deserves an enormous amount of credit for how he lifted the spirits of our franchise and our city," Ellis said.

But on March 6, Tebow's days with the Broncos became numbered as Manning's release from the Colts became a stunning reality.

The Broncos were ready.

"When a player of that magnitude becomes available, if you're not thinking about that player playing for your organization, you're not doing your fans justice," Ellis said.

During the Colts' press conference where owner Jim Irsay tearfully announced his separation from Manning, the Broncos' brain trust watched from Elway's office. Fox was in there, along with general manager Brian Xanders, personnel directors Matt Russell and Keith Kidd, and Elway. The upstairs hallways were eerily quiet.

"After Peyton was released, John (Fox) had heard through the grapevine through his contacts that there might be interest in the Broncos by Peyton," Elway said. "So that's what got the ball rolling."

Fox's primary contact was Jon Gruden, the former NFL coach who became the Monday Night Football color analyst for ESPN. Gruden had become one of Manning's closest confidantes as the quarterback went through the free-agent recruiting process. Behind-the-scenes, Gruden thought Manning would fit nicely with a team coached by Fox and run by Elway.

"You better get moving," the tipster told me. "He's coming. Today."

It was the morning of March 9, 2012. There was no reason to formally identify the pronoun. It was well understood the "he" was Peyton Manning. On March 7, *The Denver Post* broke the news that the Broncos would be among Manning's suitors. And after receiving the tip March 9, *The Denver Post* let the world know Manning was on his way to visit the Broncos at Dove Valley. By the time the story broke, Manning was sitting on Pat Bowlen's private plane on a runway in Stillwater, Oklahoma.

March 9 was a whirlwind day for the Broncos, beginning with Elway, Fox, general manager Brian Xanders, and offensive coordinator Mike McCoy attending the Oklahoma State pro-day workout that featured quarterback Brandon Weeden.

As the Broncos watched the workout, Bowlen's plane went to Miami to pick up Manning, who has a condominium in South Florida. Bowlen, meanwhile, took a red-eye flight from his Hawaii home late Thursday night, arrived in Denver early Friday morning, and was in his Dove Valley office awaiting Manning's arrival.

His private plane flew Manning back to Stillwater, where it picked up the Broncos' contingent. The Broncos' group and Manning landed about 1:35 p.m. at Centennial Airport.

After departing the plane, Manning and the Broncos contingent set off The Great Toyota Sequoia Chase. A TV camera-equipped helicopter followed the Sequoia on its slow, short ride from the airport to Broncos headquarters before the SUV disappeared into Bowlen's personal garage.

Manning spent his day visiting with Bowlen, among others, and touring the Broncos' headquarters until about 7:45 p.m. Friday night.

Manning, Elway, Fox, and Brandon Stokley – a former Colts teammate, former Broncos receiver and close friend who lived in the area – then dined at the Cherry Hills Country Club and stayed late.

Manning stayed overnight at Stokley's Castle Rock home. At about 8:30 the next morning, March 10, Manning and Stokley went to a nearby park. They brought a football along. Manning threw about 50 passes to the route-running Stokley.

That night, Stokley drove Manning to the Centennial Airport, where Manning flew on to Phoenix for a visit with the Arizona Cardinals.

Manning didn't hide his neck condition from the teams pursuing him. He put his entire medical history on a disk and gave it to all suitors. He threw for teams interested in signing him, bum neck and all.

After his visits, Manning put on throwing auditions at Duke University for the Broncos, Tennessee Titans, and San Francisco coach Jim Harbaugh.

While Elway and Tennessee Titans GM Ruston Webster sent out statements that flattered Manning's throwing audition, the executives, at best left out some truth and, at worst told a white lie.

"John said it was great," Manning said. "It wasn't great throwing. It's not supposed to be great because I'm not where I want to be. I just said, 'Here it is, guys. If you're not interested, you're not hurting my feelings. You've got to tell me.' It bothers me that I don't feel the way I want to feel. I have a lot of work to do. I'm not where I need to be."

On the morning of March 19, Fox was in Elway's office when a phone call was put through. Fox got up from his chair and started pacing. Elway was listening, then smiled broadly and raised a fist in the air.

Manning had decided to become a Bronco.

The Broncos gave him a five-year, $96 million contract, but the story was in the details. Only the first-year $18 million in salary was fully guaranteed. His $20 million salaries for 2013 and 2014 were guaranteed unless the neck prevented Manning from playing. The fourth- and fifth-year salaries of $19 million each were not guaranteed.

"I'll say this, Peyton was great about giving us protection against his neck," Elway said.

"They've got to be protected," Manning said. "That's why the whole medical – I was as open a book as I could be. I told them exactly how I feel, what I was working on. They have to know everything to make their decision.

"Even today, at the last minute, I said, 'John, put it the way you want it.' He and I talked about that from the get-go, on that first visit. You don't want to start off on a bad foot. I kind of argued with them a little bit, on their side. Nobody believes that when you say that. But it's got to be what they're comfortable with."

Manning said at his introductory press conference on March 20 his most important coaches in the next six months would be new strength-and-conditioning coach Luke Richesson and longtime trainer Steve "Greek" Antonopulos.

There was risk here. The risk was the Broncos would invest $18 million on damaged goods.

It was a risk worth taking; a risk that was rewarded many times over.

"The worst question some guys get, they ask these draft choices, 'What are you going to do with the money you just made?'" Manning said. "And they will say they're going to buy this and buy that. And I'm sitting there saying, 'I'm going to try and go earn it.'"

Kurt Warner figured out what happened with Peyton Manning.

Everybody else was amazed by what Manning accomplished despite his four neck injuries. Warner deduced Manning put together the best regular-season performance in NFL history *because* of the four neck injuries.

"I think it was a blessing in disguise going through what he went through," Warner said. "He's getting better."

A first-year starter at 28, Warner retired at 38 and is now working for the NFL Network. He was chatting with Manning off camera when he was struck with his counterintuitive theory.

Four neck injuries made Manning better? Warner said missing the entire 2011 season and getting released by Indianapolis forced Manning to start over again with the most rudimentary of quarterback fundamentals.

"I think there's always times when people say you can't do it anymore," Warner said. "Sometimes those setbacks force you to focus a little bit harder. When you talk to him about things he did during rehab – simulating games, going through every throw, making all those reads – those are things you don't do when you're healthy."

It helps explain the unexplainable. Manning, by his own admission, does not have the arm strength he had prior to his neck injury that came on late in the 2010 season. Even with the final surgery that fused his neck vertebrae together and fixed the problem to the extent it could be fixed, the nerves leading down his right arm did not fully regenerate.

He still can't grip the ball as he once did, which is why Manning – as Warner did in the final three seasons of his career in the temperature controlled Arizona dome – wears a glove on his right throwing hand, bad weather or good.

And yet Manning is better. He was a first ballot Hall of Famer during his 13 playing seasons with the Indianapolis Colts. He never put together back-to-back seasons there like he did in his first two seasons with the Broncos.

Manning nearly won the MVP award in 2012, his first with the Broncos, but finished second after a late-season surge by Adrian Peterson pushed the running back past the coveted 2,000-yard rushing milestone and his Minnesota Vikings into the playoffs.

In 2013, it was Manning who had the historic season. He garnered 49 of the 50 votes. The exception was former quarterback Jim Miller, who now co-hosts an NFL show for Sirius radio.

Miller voted for New England's Tom Brady.

Even if not by a unanimous vote, Manning had his fifth MVP award in a league where no other player had won more than three (Jim Brown, Johnny Unitas, Brett Favre).

The Broncos quarterback wound up with 55 touchdown passes, 10 percent more than the previous record of 50 set by Brady in 2007, and 5,477 yards, breaking the previous record set by Drew Brees in 2011 by 1 yard.

He led the Broncos to a 13-3 record that tied for the NFL's best record with Seattle. No one controlled the game like Manning. It is why Gruden would call him The Sheriff on his Monday Night Football broadcasts.

It was, simply, the best regular season by a quarterback in NFL history. At the NFL Honors show on Feb. 1, the MVP award was the final announcement, but drew the least suspense.

"I'm up for the honor of MVP but I'm not touching him," said Kansas City running back Jamaal Charles.

"I'd say a no-brainer right there," said New York Jets coach Rex Ryan. "I'm just happy I never had to go against him this year. I've been beat by him several times. It was good to get a break."

The MVP is a regular-season award but Manning also played well in the postseason, guiding the Broncos to home playoff wins against the division-rival San Diego Chargers, 24-17, and the more intense enemy New England Patriots, 26-16.

In those wins, Manning threw for 630 yards and four touchdowns, posting an impressive 107.1 passer rating.

Entering the Super Bowl, the question wasn't whether Manning had the best year ever. That was a given. The question was whether Manning was the best of all-time.

"I don't have a top five," said former coach Dick Vermeil. "But I do say Peyton's the best to have ever played that position. I've studied the numbers. I've taken all the numbers for the so-called great ones when they were great. His numbers are better."

Actually, Manning is second to Favre on the all-time lists in nearly every significant passing category. Manning has 64,964 passing yards – nearly 7,000 behind Favre. Manning has 5,532 completions – nearly 800 behind Favre.

It would take Manning nearly two more Manning-like years to pass Favre in those categories.

But Manning's 491 touchdown passes are only 17 behind Favre's 508. That mark should fall halfway through next season. And Favre's 336 career interceptions are so far beyond any other quarterback, it may be the only record he eventually keeps.

Even though Manning ranks second all-time in pass attempts (8,452), he is but 19th in interceptions with 219.

When it comes to the best quarterbacks of all-time, it takes a while before Favre enters the conversation.

"I don't have a list," Manning said when I asked him on the Thursday before the Super Bowl to name his top three quarterbacks of all time. "I feel like I can describe the perfect quarterback. A little piece of everybody. Take John Elway's arm, Dan Marino's release, Troy Aikman's dropback, Brett Favre's scrambling ability, Joe Montana's 2-minute poise. Naturally my speed. I can take a piece of everyone, some of my favorite quarterbacks. I can take 30 traits from different guys and put them into that perfect quarterback.

"Any time, as John Elway once said, you might be in the conversation of someone talking about this, or their favorite quarterbacks, that's a nice compliment in itself."

When I wrote my Manning legacy story for *The Denver Post* that hit driveways the Sunday morning of the Super Bowl, I said that even if he beat the Seattle Seahawks, Montana would remain No. 1.

Montana wasn't close to being the most physically gifted. Some say he benefited from playing in Bill Walsh's West Coast system, an innovative, unsolvable offense of its time.

But Manning said it when he mentioned Montana's 2-minute poise. As a quarterback, nothing beats poise under pressure. Montana was 4-0 in Super Bowls, including victories against Marino and Elway. He's No. 1.

Had Manning won the Super Bowl against the Seattle Seahawks? He may well have joined Montana as the two-best quarterbacks of all time.

Manning would only have had two Super Bowls, but he would have also been the first to win one each with two teams. So it would have been two Super Bowls with a bonus. And then he would have been the only quarterback with multiple Super Bowls and more than 400 touchdown passes.

Problem was, if Manning was going to defeat the Seahawks, he would also have to defeat history.

Manning was the fourth quarterback to reach the Super Bowl after leading the NFL in both passing yards and touchdown passes during the regular season. The others were Brady (2007), Warner (2001) and Dan Marino (1984).

Those three lost their Super Bowls by a combined score of 75-47.

The Broncos' 606 points in 2013 were the most scored by a team in a single season. Of the next eight teams on the all-time scoring list, not one went on to win the Super Bowl.

In the ultimate game, defense has ruled.

And defense prevailed again. Manning's Broncos were never in the game. The Broncos' offense created 16 points – for the Seahawks. There was a first-play bad snap leading to a safety. Manning threw a first quarter interception that led to Seattle's first touchdown. He then was clobbered as he threw in the second quarter, a deflected pass that Seattle linebacker Malcolm Smith returned for the Seahawks' second touchdown.

The last two pick sixes in Super Bowls were thrown by Manning. Legacy killers.

As a team, the Broncos didn't belong on the same field as the Seahawks. But for all of Manning's excellence, his lone Super Bowl title is baffling. Shouldn't he have lucked into at least another one or two?

Manning's overall body of work is unmatched. Again, five MVPs when no one else has more than three. But his 1-2 Super Bowl record does smudge up the way he's perceived.

Luckily for the Broncos, Manning isn't done. He is returning for a third season with the Broncos and his contract with the team doesn't end until after the 2016 season.

Manning will be 40 years old in 2016. He has dropped subtle hints along the way indicating he won't be playing at 41.

But there is still time. More time for the Broncos to win their third Super Bowl. More time for Manning to stamp his greatness.

12: 2013: Game By Incredible Game

MIKE KLIS

A new season was hours away and the city of Denver was riled. The Broncos were not only going to play their season opener against the Baltimore Ravens on a warm night at Sports Authority Field at Mile High, but the game would open up the NFL season.

The season's inaugural game should not have been played in Denver but in Baltimore's M&T Bank Stadium, home of the defending Super Bowl champion.

The Ravens, thanks to a blown coverage on a Hail Mary pass by Broncos safety Rahim Moore in a second-round playoff game the previous year, were the defending champs.

The NFL's opening night of Thursday, Sept. 5, though, had a baseball conflict. Across the parking lot from the Ravens' venue, the Orioles were to play one of 162 games against the hapless Chicago White Sox.

There isn't enough space in Camden Yards to hold two events so the Ravens had to open on the road. And the NFL schedule makers and NBC network executives thought the opener would be huge if Peyton Manning and the vengeful Broncos were the opponents.

However, the NFL, in its infinite wisdom, decided to publicize the opener as a neutral-sited game. That meant hanging posters of both Manning and Ravens' quarterback Joe Flacco – who heaved the infamous Hail Mary the last time the Broncos played – along the popular 16th Street Mall corridor in downtown Denver and on Mile High Stadium.

Denver was seething. Flacco's image was rubbing it in to Broncos fans who were still reeling from the shocking playoff loss eighth months later.

Flacco, a good-humored Joe, was relayed word how his likeness had generated seething anger from Broncos fans.

"I think it's all deserved," Flacco said. "I don't know if it's deserved towards me but I happen to be the guy they put up there. I don't think people here or anybody in our city would be too happy if we had somebody else from a different team on our stadium. I wouldn't expect anything different but all the people in Denver to be pretty upset about it."

And so the scene was set for the Broncos to open their 2013 season against the Ravens at hostile Sports Authority Field and Mile High.

Game 1 (1-0)	**Broncos 49** **Ravens 27**	Thursday, Sept. 5 Denver, CO
Manning Stats	27 of 42 462 yards	7 TDs, 0 INTs
Breakout Player	Julius Thomas TE	Shaun Philips DE
Key Injury	Champ Bailey LCB	

In Manning's first regular season game since he turned 37 years old, he threw not one, not two, not three or four touchdown passes. Manning threw seven. He also passed for 462 yards.

Game 1 would catapult Manning to a record-setting category in both touchdown yards and passing touchdowns.

"I mean, shoot, he's almost halfway to 20, already," Flacco said.

Manning was the sixth NFL quarterback in history to throw seven TD passes in a game, the first since Joe Kapp in a 1969 game against the Baltimore Colts.

"Yeah, Joe Kapp, right?" said Manning in his postgame press conference. "The great Canadian quarterback out of Cal. He kicked the crap out of a guy on YouTube a couple years ago, too.

"You never know what's going to happen in a game. I felt like we had to keep scoring. Baltimore is an explosive offense." Among the many lessons the Broncos learned from their heartbreaking, 38-35 double overtime loss in the previous season's playoffs, was that they have to keep scoring.

Manning spread his completions around so that newcomer Wes Welker and top-returning receiver Demaryius Thomas would have big days but the favorite early target was Julius Thomas.

I remember the first time I saw Julius. It was during the lockout summer of 2011 and sports performance trainer Loren Landow was working with the Broncos' players who were not allowed to be at the Broncos' training facilities, or be coached by any of the team's employees.

So with veteran safety Brian Dawkins at the forefront, the Broncos organized their own workouts. Thomas showed up on June 28, the only member of the Broncos' 2011 rookie class who demonstrated the initiative to work out with the locked out veterans.

Following the 45-minute conditioning session on his first day, Thomas ran patterns for veteran quarterback Brady Quinn. Thomas is 6-foot-5, 250 pounds and moves with the athleticism of a basketball power forward, which is what he was for four years at Portland State. He didn't play football until his senior year.

Starting with Tony Gonzalez in 1997, the league had become infatuated with converting power forwards into tight ends.

"Some of the things that translate from basketball to football are a little bit of a misconception. The athleticism is what translates. What doesn't translate is pad level," Thomas said after the Broncos' workout at Valor Christian High School. "In basketball, you try to play as tall as possible. In football, you're trying to play as low as possible. Football is a unique sport in that way."

The Broncos selected Julius Thomas in the fourth round of the 2011 draft, knowing he was a raw project who would have to develop blocking skills.

But during the lockout session, Thomas opened eyes from his first seam-pattern catch from Quinn.

"If I was a coach," Landow said, "I'd never have him block."

It took Thomas a while to develop. He suffered a severe ankle injury while making his first NFL catch for 5 yards in the Broncos' second game against Cincinnati. He essentially missed the rest of the 2011 and 2012 seasons, with the exception of a few special teams' assignments.

Thomas had just the one NFL catch entering this third season. In the opener against Baltimore, he had two touchdown receptions in the first half.

The Broncos played this game without star cornerback Champ Bailey, who had not recovered from his sprained Lisfranc injury in his left foot suffered during a preseason game at Seattle. A 12-time Pro Bowler, Bailey would miss 11 games this season.

As a subplot, this game featured the return of defensive end Elvis Dumervil. The Broncos' best pass rusher from the time he was selected in the fourth round of the 2006 draft until Von Miller became the team's No. 2 overall pick in the 2011 draft, Dumervil left the team and signed with the Ravens under the most bizarre of circumstances.

The Broncos wanted to cut Dumervil's salary from $14 million in 2013 to $6.5 million. The Broncos eventually came up to $8 million but Dumervil balked until about 20 minutes remaining in the free-agent deadline period, when he accepted.

Too late. By the time the official documents were exchanged by fax, the two sides missed the deadline. Dumervil was officially released to free agency and he spurned another make-good offer by the Broncos to sign with Baltimore.

The Broncos replaced him by signing Shaun Phillips, who had been a trash-talking, Broncos killer the previous nine seasons as a pass-rushing linebacker for the rival San Diego Chargers.

In Phillips' first game for the Broncos, he registered 2 ½ sacks against Flacco.

Game 2 (2-0)	Broncos 41 Giants 23	Sunday, Sept. 15 East Rutherford, NJ
Manning Stats	30 of 43 307 yards	2 TDs, 0 INTs
Breakout Player	Knowshon Moreno RB	
Key Injury	Ryan Clady LT	

Peyton Manning against his younger brother Eli, quarterback of the New York Giants, in East Rutherford, NJ– site of Super Bowl XLVIII.

This game was billed as Manning Bowl III. Although Eli had led the Giants to two Super Bowl titles – one more championship ring than Peyton – the older brother is considered the better of the two.

Manning III ended with the same result as I and II – Peyton's team winning decisively.

"I'd take Peyton over anybody, not just Eli. That's any quarterback ever," said Broncos defensive tackle Terrance Knighton.

Peyton was again brilliant in the second half while Eli threw four interceptions. Peyton finished the season with the most touchdown passes (55); Eli finished with the most interceptions (27).

What helped Peyton was the Broncos' front line was able to set up the running game for Knowshon Moreno. While Denver's defense held the Giants to 23 yards rushing on 19 carries, Moreno emerged as a fantasy darling.

Long considered a first-round bust after then-Broncos football boss Josh McDaniels took him with the No. 12 overall pick in the

2009 draft, Moreno was inactive by coach's decision for eight games in 2012, but finished strong after starter Willis McGahee went down with a broken leg injury.

Against the Giants, Moreno scored on identical-looking, right-end sweeps – the first for 20 yards and the second for 25.

"You don't have to go outside yourself and try to make plays," Moreno said. "You just have to go out there, do the keys, make sure you're doing the right thing, and those things will come."

For all the positive in the Broncos' first road win of the season, though, there would be a setback: Ryan Clady became the first in a long line of standout Bronco players to suffer a season-ending injury.

Late in the game, as the Broncos were running out the clock, the All Pro left tackle who had just received a five-year, $52.5 million contract in July, suffered a torn Lisfranc in his left foot. Clady received $15 million in salary and signing bonus in 2013. He played in just two games.

He was replaced the rest of the season by Chris Clark, who spent his first two NFL seasons on Minnesota's practice squad, and next three as the Broncos' backup tackle. In year six, Chris Clark would be charged with protecting Peyton Manning's blindside.

Game 3 (3-0)	**Broncos 37** **Raiders 21**	Monday, Sept. 23 Denver, CO
Manning Stats	32 of 37 374 yards	3 TDs, 0 INTs
Breakout Player	Eric Decker WR	
Key Injury	N/A	

This was Peyton having fun in the Garden District of New Orleans, teasing all his no-hope hometown chums in a game of two-hand touch.

With 2 minutes left in the first half of the Broncos' early romp against a confused collection of Oakland Raiders on Monday night, Manning was 18 of 20 for 229 yards and 3 touchdown passes. Couldn't call him perfect because his two incompletions were drops.

His favorite target was Eric Decker, who had 8 catches for 133 yards and his first touchdown. Decker badly needed this game. With his GQ coverboy looks and down-home personality, Decker was an NFL star who had it all.

He also had country-pop singer Jessie James as his fiancée. Not only did the celebrity couple wed in June, their off-field romance became the subject of an E! reality series. *Eric & Jessie: Game On* would debut the following week following Game 4 against the Philadelphia Eagles.

"I'm not nervous about it," Decker said Friday in the locker room at Broncos headquarters. "I decided to do it, so why be nervous? I realize it might change as far as going out and doing things. But we still feel like normal people."

The reality show drew mixed reviews, but it also magnified the spotlight on Decker. And early on, he was singed. Decker had four drops in his first two games.

Suddenly, he was a little too Hollywood. Too absorbed in outside interests.

The Raiders game quieted such chatter. Decker finished the season among the top 12 in the NFL with 87 catches for 1,288 yards and 11 touchdowns.

The previous season, the year before a cable-viewing audience peeked in on him and Jessie James, and the year before the Broncos added Julius Thomas and Wes Welker to Manning's arsenal, Decker had 85 catches for 1,064 yards and 13 touchdowns.

Nothing hurt.

Game 4 (4-0)	Broncos 52 Eagles 20	Sunday, Sept. 29 Denver, CO
Manning Stats	28 of 34 327 yards	4 TDs, 0 INTs
Breakout Player	Demaryius Thomas WR	Wes Welker WR
Key Injury	N/A	

The hype to this game centered around first-year Eagles coach Chip Kelly, who was bringing his fast-tempo, high-scoring offensive system from the college ranks and the Oregon Ducks.

The Broncos jumped out quickly as Manning finished off a systemic first drive with the first of his two touchdown passes to Wes Welker. He didn't get a second drive as Trindon Holliday returned a kickoff 105 yards for a touchdown.

Manning threw 16 touchdown passes with zero interceptions through 4 games. Not since Milt Plum in 1960 had a quarterback started the season with those numbers. The difference is it took Plum 10 games to throw his 16. And he threw an interception later in Game 10.

"I'm throwing out 16 as his (uniform) number – is that right?" Manning said correctly. "My brother Cooper and I used to play a lot of trivia when we used to take road trips with my dad. So Cooper would be proud that I did know Plum."

As Manning walked away from the podium in his postgame news conference, he was asked if he remembered Sammy Baugh's number. Momentarily, Manning said No. 42, but he soon realized that was Sid Luckman's number. Manning has been passing so many greats in recent weeks, it was getting difficult to keep them straight.

"No. 33," Manning said correctly of Baugh's number.

By winning all 15 games by at least seven points, Manning's Broncos have the longest such streak since the Luckman-quarterbacked Chicago Bears won 16 in a row by such margins in 1941 and 1942.

Manning's 16 touchdown passes through four games broke the NFL record of 14 touchdown passes set by Baugh in 1943 and tied by Don Meredith in 1966 and Warner in 1999.

Sorry, Slingin' Sammy. After 70 years, that four-game TD record no longer belongs to No. 33.

Before Manning signed to play with the Broncos before the 2012 season, he already was considered one of the all-time best quarterbacks. In the 20 regular-season games since he has donned bright orange, Manning has been absurd, leading the Broncos to 17 victories on 53 touchdown passes against only 11 interceptions. He had gone to a level through four games this season that not even the greatest of the greats had gone before.

Imagine the pressure that was on quarterback Michael Vick and the Eagles' offense. They had it going for a while, drawing within 14-13 early in the second quarter. But the Eagles stopped scoring. And the Broncos scored the next 38 points.

Manning didn't play in the fourth quarter as backup Brock Osweiler got some playing time with the Broncos up 49-13.

The 52 points was one of several franchise records the Broncos set.

"I did not know that," said Manning, showing an apparent trivia weakness beyond the national realm. "Might have to give Thunder an IV after that one."

The Broncos' four-legged gelding has been busy running around the field after Denver touchdowns since his team brought in Manning to lead. The victory Sunday was the Broncos' 15th in a row during the regular season, breaking the franchise record on a day when Tom Nalen was inducted into the Ring of Fame. Nalen was the starting center on the 1997 and 1998 Broncos who won 14 in a row. John Elway was the starting quarterback for most of that streak.

Manning broke into the NFL as its No. 1 draft choice in 1998 and it's gone long past the point where he has been considered a legend in his own time. It's only right that one of the cherished records he had next in his sights is one engineered by Manning himself.

The NFL record of 23 consecutive regular-season games was set by the 2008-09 Indianapolis Colts. You know who quarterbacked that team.

Future quarterbacks had better know No. 18.

Game 5 (5-0)	**Broncos 51** **Cowboys 48**	Sunday, Oct. 6 Arlington, TX
Manning Stats	33 of 42 414 yards	4 TDs, 1 INT
Breakout Player	Julius Thomas TE	Knowshon Moreno RB
Key Injury	Wesley Woodyard LB	

This was the most entertaining game of the season. Certainly not the best for the Broncos – their flaws on defense were exposed. But you couldn't beat the action.

Manning and Romo combined for 920 yards passing, 9 touchdown passes and 99 points.

Manning won. Besides his four touchdown passes, he ran in a touchdown off a brilliant fake handoff, naked bootleg keep from the 1-inch line. Cowboys' right defensive end DeMarcus Ware, who following this season signed with the Broncos, crashed into the middle where running back Montee Ball didn't have the ball.

Peyton pranced alone to the left side of the end zone. It was his first rushing touchdown in five years.

Manning was the talk of the league. The Broncos were 5-0 and he had thrown his 17th, 18th, 19th, and 20th touchdown passes of the season – each one a record – before a deep ball thrown into a sunny opening at AT&T Stadium caused receiver Eric Decker to lose the ball for a moment and led to his first interception of the season.

Apologies to the rest of the Broncos. They all do their part. But this season was all about Manning.

"Hey, I get it," said Broncos slot man Wes Welker, who also was part of Tom Brady's record-setting offenses in New England. "He's a great player. You can't take anything away from him. You don't mind talking about the quarterback when they play like that."

Leading up to the game, Cowboys veteran linebacker Ernie Sims was quoted as saying he was sick of hearing about Manning.

"I think I might have caught a glimpse of that on ESPN or something, but that wasn't anything we used for motivation or anything," said Broncos tight end Julius Thomas. "You're going to hear about Peyton when he's playing like that. What did he throw, four again today? Well, guess what. He'll be back on the news again."

Julius Thomas had his best game with 9 catches for 122 yards and 2 touchdowns. Knowshon Moreno was sensational, gaining 93 yards rushing on 19 carries and catching 5 passes for 57 yards.

Perhaps the biggest yard of the game, though, was the yard Moreno didn't gain.

The score was 48-48 when Romo spoiled his brilliant day – he was a Houdini against pressure and threw for 506 yards and 5 touchdowns – by throwing into triple coverage deep in his own end. Broncos linebacker Danny Trevathan made a diving interception and the Broncos were in business at the Cowboys' 24.

Two Manning completions and the Broncos had the ball third-and-1 at the Cowboys 2. There was 1 minute, 35 seconds remaining – too much time for Romo's Cowboys to answer a Broncos' touchdown.

Manning turned to Moreno and made one unusual request: gain 1 yard for a first down, but don't gain 2 yards for a touchdown. That way, with the first down, the Broncos could run out the clock before Matt Prater kicked an easy field goal.

Moreno could be seen visibly arguing with Manning in the huddle. "I can't do that," Moreno said. "How can I gain one yard and not two?"

"You have to," Manning said.

Moreno came through. He fought for 1 yard, then fell before the goal line. Manning took three knees, called a timeout and with 2 seconds remaining, Matt Prater kicked a short, game-winning field goal.

There was a disturbing aspect to the win. The Broncos' defense, particularly in the secondary, was atrocious. Nickel cornerback Tony Carter was benched after this game and didn't really play meaningful cornerback snaps until the AFC Championship.

Middle linebacker Wesley Woodyard also received a concussion and neck stinger in the first half and didn't return. The neck stinger would eventually lead Woodyard – the defensive captain – to the bench. He would be replaced at the middle linebacker position by Paris Lenon, a 36-year-old journeyman, but also a nine-year starter.

Game 6 (6-0)	**Broncos 35** **Jaguars 19**	Sunday, Oct. 13 Denver, CO
Manning Stats	28 of 42 295 yards	2 TDs, 1 INTs
Breakout Player	Malik Jackson DE	
Key Injury	Peyton Manning QB	Orlando Franklin RT

You know what they say: It's hard to play when you're laughing. When the week opened, the 5-0 Broncos were all-time, regular-season record 27 ½-point favorites against the 0-5 Jacksonville Jaguars.

As the Broncos' own web site tweeted out, the Jags had scored 51 points all year. The Broncos scored 51 points in their previous game against the Cowboys.

The Jacksonville Jaguars' Twitter handle retweeted the Broncos' message and added, "Stay classy, Denver."

The Broncos apologized, then quickly jumped out to a 14-0 lead on two Manning touchdown passes on their first two possessions before seemingly growing bored.

Then came the reminder that no team can take another team lightly, even when it's the best team against the worst. The overconfident Broncos lost their focus. And the Jaguars stumbled their way back into the game. Manning threw his first pick six of the season late in the first half, as Jags middle linebacker Paul Posluszny, a terrific player, dropped deep in his Tampa 2 zone coverage. Posluszny snared the Manning pass and returned it 59 yards for a touchdown.

Jacksonville hung tough until midway through the third quarter, exchanging touchdowns with the Broncos to make it 21-19. But Moreno scored two short rushing touchdowns to put it away.

But this would be one of Manning's three-worst regular-season games of the year. Besides the pick six, he lost two fumbles and settled in below 300 passing yards.

He also was wrapped up around his right ankle after delivering a pass from his end zone in the first half. Manning wound up with a high ankle sprain that was treated the rest of the season but never caused him to miss a snap.

In the second half, the Broncos lost massive right tackle Orlando Franklin to a left knee injury. Louis Vasquez, a 60-game NFL starter at guard, shifted over one spot to right tackle in the second half, while Chris Kuper was inserted to his old right guard position.

Kuper had been a starting Broncos guard from 2007 until he gruesomely dislocated his left ankle in the final game of the 2011 season. He never recovered, although he was a part-time starter for two more seasons.

On the defensive side, it was a big game for second-year defensive end Malik Jackson. A fifth-round pick out of Tennessee in the 2012 draft, Jackson played sparingly as a rookie before getting rotated in on nickel situations in his second season. He had several near-misses and 1 ½ sacks through his first five games, before he twice dumped Jacksonville quarterback Chad Henne in this one.

Game 7 (6-1)	Colts 39 Broncos 33	Sunday, Oct. 20 Indianapolis, IN
Manning Stats	29 of 49 386 yards	3 TDs, 1 INTs
Breakout Player	Von Miller LB	
Key Injury	N/A	

This was supposed to be Peyton Manning's highly anticipated homecoming.

Peyton Manning, and Peyton Manning alone, put Indianapolis on the national sports map (perhaps with an assist, in the form of a deep trey, from Reggie Miller).

After all Manning had done for the Colts – 11.5 wins a season in the 12-year period from 1999-2010, 11 playoff appearances, two AFC titles, one Super Bowl title, civic pride boost to build a new stadium – the Colts were going to welcome him back with a video tribute and presumably a standing ovation.

Only Colts owner Jim Irsay couldn't help himself.

In an interview with USA Today, Irsay started off by saying nice things about Manning, but then, maybe because Manning was play-ing far better than anyone thought possible since Irsay released him in March 2012, the Colts owner seemed to defend his decision.

"We've changed our model a little bit, because we wanted more than one of these," Irsay told the paper while flicking up his right hand to show his Super Bowl XLI championship ring.

That Super Bowl ring, by the way, was delivered thanks to Manning's Super Bowl MVP performance in a driving Miami rain.

"(Tom) Brady never had consistent numbers, but he has three of these," Irsay adds. "Pittsburgh had two, the Giants had two, Baltimore had two, and we had one. That leaves you frustrated...You make the playoffs 11 times, and you're out in the first round seven out of 11 times. You love to have the Star Wars numbers from Peyton and Marvin (Harrison) and Reggie (Wayne). Mostly, you love this."

Then, according to the USA Today article, Irsay flicked up his right hand again.

It was a classless gesture that marred Manning's return.

Look, everyone knows Manning has just one Super Bowl title and what is now an 11-12 playoff record. But a missed field goal cost him one year. Bad defense cost him some others. A 70-yard Hail Mary cost him last year.

The tribute went on despite Irsay and Manning took time to thank the crowd. He then played well early, finishing off his first drive with a 17-yard touchdown pass to Decker, who finished with 8 catches for 150 yards.

But in the second quarter, and the Broncos operating near their own end zone, Colts defensive end Robert Mathis blew past left tackle Chris Clark.

Mathis delivered a blindside wallop on his former teammate Manning, resulting in not only a sack-fumble-safety, but altered momentum.

The Colts, behind second-year quarterback Andrew Luck – the man who replaced Manning – went up 33-14 with five minutes left in the 3rd quarter.

Showing the type of greatness that should not be easily discarded, and never, ever diminished by a loquacious owner whose team is about to play him, Manning nearly rallied the Broncos to an improbable comeback.

Denver got within 36-30 and had the ball at its 15-yard line with seven minutes left. But on first down, Manning had his arm hit as he threw and his pass was intercepted. Indianapolis soon after kicked a field goal for a 39-30 lead. The Broncos subsequently drove to the Colts' 2-yard line before Ronnie Hillman fumbled on first down, with the Colts recovering with just over three minutes left, all but sealing the victory.

Still, Manning took the high road. He said he had put Irsay's comments behind him and thanked him for the tribute.

"In some ways, I feel relieved this game is over," Manning said.

The outcome spoiled another return – that of linebacker Von Miller to the Broncos. Sensational while recording 30 quarterback sacks in his first two seasons, Miller returned to the Broncos' lineup after serving a six-game suspension for violating the NFL's drug policy.

Usually, such an offense draws a four-game suspension, but Miller had aggravated his situation by allegedly trying to provide a false sample to a urine collector in cahoots.

Against the Colts, Miller played relatively strong against the run and applied pressure on Luck, but didn't come up with an impact play.

Game 8 (7-1)	**Broncos 45** **Redskins 21**	Sunday, Oct. 27 Denver, CO
Manning Stats	30 of 44 354 yards	4 TDs, 3 INTs
Breakout Player	Dominique Rodgers- Cromartie CB	
Key Injury	N/A	

When Redskins coach Mike Shanahan returned to Denver, his high-end steakhouse restaurant and 35,000-square-foot mansion in Cherry Hills Village were waiting for him.

In 2007, while he was still coaching the Broncos, Shanahan moved into the mansion he built as his restaurant was opening. Although he was, and remains, the Broncos' all-time winningest coach, he was fired after the 2008 season following a third consecutive season without a playoff appearance.

Shanahan kept the mansion and the restaurant even after he took the Redskins job prior to the 2010 season.

"Well, remember, I didn't know I was getting fired," Shanahan said. "With the market the way it is, sometimes you keep homes and sometimes you let them go. But we felt like with the kids being raised there and still a lot of family going back and forth, we kept the house and I'm glad we did."

For the first time since he was fired following the 2008 season, Shanahan returned to Denver coaching for another team. He showed up on the hot seat as his Redskins were 2-4 and second-year quarterback Robert Griffin III was playing ineffectively.

Surprisingly, the Redskins jumped out to a 21-7 lead as Manning was intercepted three times, including a pick six by Leon Hall, and lost a fumble.

But the Redskins imploded with turnovers in the second half. Manning threw two 35-yard touchdown passes in the second half and cornerback Dominique Rodgers-Cromartie iced the game with a high-stepping, 75-yard touchdown return off a Kirk Cousins interception.

Shanahan wound up getting fired at the end of the year.

Game 9 (8-1)	**Broncos 28** **Chargers 20**	Sunday, Nov. 10 San Diego, CA
Manning Stats	25 of 36 330 yards	4 TDs, 0 INTs
Breakout Player	Demaryius Thomas WR	Jack Del Rio Interim Head Coach
Key Injury	John Fox Head Coach	

Every Friday morning, from about 6:45 until his weekly radio show with 850 KOA begins at 7:20, John Fox lets his players know he is not just their head coach. He is one of them.

He hangs out in the trainers' room for a few minutes, exchanging jokes and stories. He'll visit the team chow hall and sit down with a group of players. He'll work the locker room.

Unlike Miami's Joe Philbin, who allowed a horrific bullying incident to occur under his watch, Fox is like the good doctor with the bedside manner and a stethoscope on his team's pulse.

Former Broncos coach Mike Shanahan could win games on Sunday through his game plan. Fox wins games through his work Monday through Saturday.

It was during their midseason break that the Broncos' temporarily lost their leader. Without a prayer to God and a lucky break with logistics, the Broncos may have lost Fox, period.

The Broncos were 7-1 at the bye week when the team and its employees dispersed for a four-day break. Football operations boss John Elway was at the Breeder's Cup in California when he got the call that Fox had an episode on a golf course in Charlotte, N.C. and was getting his heart checked out at a local hospital.

"The idea he would have to have this surgery was not new to me," Elway said. "So I was glad to hear that when something happened on the golf course that he was safe and sound."

Safe but it took a little more doing before his heart was sound.

Fox had known since 1997 his heart had a genetic valve defect where there were only two flaps instead of the usual three.

Over time, those overworked flaps would calcify, making it a little harder for each heart beat to move blood to where it needed to go.

Fox had meetings with cardiologists every year since his irregularity was discovered. And yet Fox was out there every single week for five seasons as defensive coordinator with the New York Giants, nine seasons as head coach of the Carolina Panthers, and halfway through his third season with the Broncos – yelling at officials, exhorting his players, leading his coaching staff and making crucial game-deciding decisions.

Talk about courage. Talk about a guy dedicated to his craft.

"My wife, Robin, would say, 'stupid,'" Fox said.

In June, as the Broncos were about to conduct their final mini-camp practice session of the offseason, Fox was told valve replacement surgery was needed no later than the end of this season.

"I made a poor health decision at that time," Fox said.

He put it off until the end of the season. Halfway through, Fox visited his cardiologist in Raleigh, N.C. on Halloween, a Thursday, then played golf two days later with some of his buddies at the Charlotte golf course right outside his back door.

He was on the 14th hole – the hole his house overlooks – when he started feeling faint. After putting out, he laid down on the back of the green.

"When I was on my knees on the golf course, I remember praying to God, 'You get me out of this and I'll get it fixed,'" Fox told Mark Kiszla of *The Denver Post*. "That's how scary it was… It was like being smothered. I couldn't breathe."

He was taken to a nearby hospital, where doctors said he would need open-heart surgery to replace the aortic valve in two days, Monday, Nov. 4.

"Coach Fox is in our prayers right now," said Broncos' tight end Joel Dreessen. "He's our leader. We love him. If you know anything about him, you know he'll be just fine."

Before Fox went in for his surgery, he entered into an agreement with his doctors and Broncos.

"We told him you can talk to guys all you want, but you're staying away for four weeks," Elway said.

Fox was 58 with a wife and kids young enough to need their father. So he wasn't going to do anything silly. But the four-week mandate was difficult for a guy who lived with his heart condition for 16 years.

Fox's medical leave occurred during the most difficult quarter of the Broncos' schedule. It started with game 9 at San Diego. Needing a new head coach, Elway didn't overthink it.

Jack Del Rio became the Broncos' defensive coordinator in 2012 after he had spent nine seasons as head coach of the Jacksonville Jaguars.

Del Rio was the obvious choice. Under difficult circumstances, he was steady yet flexible. Excited for the opportunity, he didn't overwhelm the players with speeches or changes. Manning, among others, was impressed.

In a key AFC West matchup on the road, Manning ended his mini, midseason "slump." Manning had failed to post a passer rating of at least 100.0 in his three previous games, as he threw five interceptions in that span.

Rejuvenated by the bye week, Manning was near flawless against the Chargers, posting a 135.2 rating. Three of his four touchdown passes went to Demaryius Thomas; the other went to Julius Thomas.

The game wasn't as close as the final score made it appear as the Broncos went up 28-6 midway through the third quarter. Chargers coach Mike McCoy – Manning's offensive coordinator the previous year in Denver – devised a ball-control game plan where Manning's offense only had the ball for 22 minutes of the 60-minute game.

But Manning and the Broncos made the most of their limited chances. The ugly moments in victory were two Charger licks on Manning, who came away limping badly on his sore right ankle. Blindsided in the third quarter by outside linebacker Tourek Williams, who beat left tackle Chris Clark on the play, Manning fumbled as he was sacked and the turnover helped the Chargers make a game of it.

"I hate these fumbles but they are all when I'm throwing," Manning said. "I'm conscious of protecting it when I'm in the pocket but ... I haven't quite figured out how to not fumble when they hit you while you're not throwing."

Manning's right ankle injury was aggravated on his final, game-clinching completion when he was struck low by Chargers' defensive end Corey Liuget.

Manning didn't practice on Wednesdays the rest of the regular season as he received treatment on his right ankle.

Game 10 (9-1)	**Broncos 27** **Chiefs 17**	Sunday, Nov. 17 Denver, CO
Manning Stats	24 of 40 323 yards	1 TD, 0 INTs
Breakout Player	Shaun Philips DE	
Key Injury	Rahim Moore S Wes Welker SR	Julius Thomas TE

As the season unfolded, it became increasingly apparent this Broncos-Chiefs matchup was going to be the biggest game of the regular season.

The surprising Chiefs entered this game with a 9-0 record – after finishing with the NFL's worst mark the previous year at 2-14. What a difference a head coach and quarterback make.

Andy Reid had nine playoff appearances from 2000-2010 with the Philadelphia Eagles, reaching the Super Bowl in the 2004 season. Alex Smith had quarterbacked the San Francisco 49ers to a 19-5-1 record in 2011 and 2012, when he suffered an injury that led to Colin Kaepernick. Smith had been Wally Pipp'ed.

This was the first game of the 2013 season that Manning wore a glove on his right passing hand. The temperature at game time was 43°. It would fall into the 30s in the second half. Manning would wear the glove the rest of the season, even in warm weather.

Still ailing with a sore right ankle and the Chiefs' defense bringing an NFL-most 36 sacks into the game, Manning did more handing off than usual. He did throw a 70-yard completion to Demaryius Thomas that set up a 9-yard touchdown pass to Julius Thomas – the tight end's 10th scoring reception of the season.

The keys to the game, though, were a first-and-goal stand by the Denver defense to hold the Chiefs to a field goal, and linebacker Danny Trevathan forcing a fumble deep in Broncos' territory one play after Manning fumbled a handoff exchange with running back Montee Ball.

The win moved the Broncos into a first-place tie with the Chiefs at 9-1. But this was also a game that started an unfortunate string of injuries.

First, tight end Julius Thomas suffered a knee injury in the third quarter that forced him to miss the next two weeks.

Second, slot receiver Wes Welker suffered a concussion in the fourth quarter. He was walloped after a catch-and-run for a 20-yard gain across the middle and lay on the field for a spell. The Broncos' medical team of doctors and trainer Steve "Greek" Antonopulos saw how Welker's head was snapped back and it was his neck that was evaluated.

No concussion symptoms were apparent. On the sideline, Welker shook off the neck and the Broncos cleared him to go back in. He made a 9-yard catch to finish the Broncos' drive that ended with a Matt Prater field goal. It was after that series that Welker began experiencing a headache, a possible concussion-like symptom that removed him from the game.

Welker returned the next week to play against his former New England Patriots, but later in the season, he would suffer another concussion. The second one was treated with greater caution.

Meanwhile, free safety Rahim Moore, who was enjoying a nice bounce-back season from his late-game playoff stumble against Jacoby Jones and the Ravens, had been feeling pain in his lower left leg since early in the week.

He had played all 73 defensive snaps in his team's win at San Diego the previous week so he thought he was experiencing nothing other than post-game aches and pains – even if the soreness was hanging around a little longer than usual.

"It was like Wednesday and Thursday. There was something, but it was minor," Moore said. "As the week went on, it got better and better. So I thought, 'OK, it's nothing.'"

But during warm-ups for the Chiefs game, Moore's left leg experienced weakness.

"Then the first two series, I didn't feel it at all," he said. "It must have been the adrenaline, whatever. But then after a while, I started realizing I wasn't fast enough to help my team play on certain runs and certain reads I should make."

He came out of the game with a condition that was a mystery to the Broncos' medical team. Moore, 23, went to bed that night, but couldn't sleep because of numbness in his left foot and lower leg.

Moore called Keith Bishop, the former Broncos offensive guard who now heads the team's security department. Bishop called trainer "Greek" Antonopulos, who called Moore with orders to get to the nearest hospital to get checked out.

"Really, I just went in to get some pain meds," Moore said. "But the pain meds didn't do anything. It just got worse and worse as we waited. They stuck a needle in there to tell whether I had too much pressure or not, and they told me I needed surgery."

Moore was suffering from a condition called lateral compartment syndrome. Moore argued against surgery with the doctors until they informed him of the grave consequences he faced.

"I was scared they were going to have to amputate my leg; that's what I was most scared of," Moore said. "But God is great. None of that happened."

The Broncos placed Moore on injured reserve with a designation to return in hopes he could play in the AFC championship game and

Super Bowl, providing they made it that far. The team did but Moore could not. It was the first of three consecutive games in which the Broncos lost a defensive starter to a season-ending injury.

Game 11 (9-2)	**Patriots 34** **Broncos 31**	Sunday, Nov 24 Foxborough, MA
Manning Stats	19 of 36 150 yards	2 TDs, 1 INT
Breakout Player	Knowshon Moreno RB	Jacob Tamme TE Von Miller SLB
Key Injury	Kevin Vickerson DT	Dominique Rodgers-Cormartie CB

This was Manning's worst statistical game of the year but there was an explanation: 22° temperatures with 22 mph winds. Mix them together and it computes to a 6° wind-chill.

Knowing the blustery conditions well in advance, Broncos offensive coordinator Adam Gase put together a run-heavy game plan. Patriots coach Bill Belichick, meanwhile, devised a defense that took away Manning's top receivers, Demaryius Thomas and Eric Decker, who combined for just five catches and 46 yards.

The Patriots often had just six defenders in the box area, sometimes only five, even four.

Between the Broncos' emphasizing the run and the Pats' de-emphasizing stopping the run, Knowshon Moreno ran wild.

The fifth-year running back rushed for 224 yards off a yeoman-like 37 carries, easily the best game of his career.

Meanwhile, Denver's defense had its best one-half effort of the season, forcing three Patriots turnovers. Von Miller, in easily the best game of his otherwise disappointing season, returned a Wesley Woodyard-forced fumble for a 60-yard touchdown that opened the scoring.

Miller wound up with two sacks, the first time since his suspension that he resembled the disruptive force of his first two seasons.

When Manning threw a 10-yard touchdown pass to Jacob Tamme, who was filling in for Julius Thomas at tight end, the Broncos had a 24-0 lead at halftime.

The final play of the first half was a bad break for the Broncos. A Hail Mary pass by Brady was held up by the wind and Broncos cornerback Dominique Rodgers-Cromartie made a play on it. Inexplicably given the zero time remaining, Rodgers-Cromartie dove for the ball that fell harmlessly to the turf. Or not so harmlessly. Rodgers-Cromartie wound up with a badly bruised shoulder but no interception. He didn't return in the second half as Brady lit up the Broncos' secondary and Rodgers-Cromartie would also miss the following week's AFC West showdown at Kansas City.

The Broncos gagged away the rest of the game. Anytime there is an inexcusable meltdown, or miraculous-type comeback, at least one key turnover is always involved.

In this case, the Broncos committed two – a fumble by rookie running back Montee Ball and a poorly thrown interception into the wind by Manning.

Each turnover led to a short-field touchdown drive by the Patriots and Tom Brady, who was remarkable in the second half despite the inclement conditions. Playing catch-up from middle of the second quarter on, Brady completed 34 of 50 passes for 344 yards, three touchdown passes and no interceptions.

Once again, Brady beat Manning. The difference this time is Manning seemed to have the better team.

In fairness to Manning, he did not lose this one. He led the Broncos on a 19-play, 80-yard touchdown drive in the fourth quarter to tie it, 31-31. In overtime, a fluke play cost the Broncos.

Wes Welker, employed as a punt returner since the Broncos didn't trust Trindon Holliday to field the ball in windy conditions, backed away at the last second from fielding a punt deep in his own end. The ball ricocheted right into the Broncos' Tony Carter, who was flying down for a block.

Ball! The Pats recovered and kicked a short field goal for the win.

"I was blocking my guy to try to spring Wes (Welker) for a return," Carter said after the game. "I heard the 'Peter' call which means everyone get out of the way. I tried to get out of the way, but the ball bounced right into me. Tough bounce."

The Broncos lost their defensive front leader in this game as tackle Kevin Vickerson suffered a dislocated hip, an injury that finished his season. Vickerson had been the Broncos' best interior defensive lineman.

When he left, Terrance Knighton stepped up into a starring role while first-round rookie Sylvester Williams took Vickerson's spot at left defensive tackle.

Game 12 (10-2)	**Broncos 35** **Chiefs 28**	Sunday, Dec. 1 Kansas City, MO
Manning Stats	22 of 35 403 yards	5 TDs, 2 INTs
Breakout Player	Eric Decker WR	Montee Ball RB
Key Injury	Derek Wolfe DE	

Peyton Manning became the Mad Bomber.

Arm strength had been a question for the 37-year-old quarterback since he missed the 2011 season to recover from four neck surgeries. It became a discussion topic again when he threw for a season-low 150 yards in frigid, windy conditions at New England.

But in this game, the second in three weeks against the Chiefs, Manning flexed and heaved.

He connected on touchdown passes of 41 and 37 yards to Eric Decker, who torched the Chiefs' man-to-man, press covering cornerbacks for four touchdowns. On another series, a 42-yard completion to Decker set up a short touchdown toss to running back Knowshon Moreno.

On another drive, a 77-yard strike-and-run with Demaryius Thomas set up a 15-yard scoring zinger to Decker.

"I don't measure the length of the throws," Manning said. "Sometimes when you play a team close to back-to-back, there are some ideas you wish you could've got to in that first game that you can get to in that second game.

"We thought there were some chances to get down the field in that first game that we never got to. I thought Adam was aggressive and called some deep shots at the right time."

The road trip got off to an inauspicious start. As the Broncos' buses left Dove Valley and headed to the Denver International Airport, second-year defensive lineman Derek Wolfe was stricken by a seizure-like episode. Medical people helped get Wolfe off the bus and in the back of an ambulance – his second emergency medical ride of the season. Wolfe had also suffered a neck injury during a preseason game Aug. 17 at Seattle and was immobilized on the field.

He recovered from the neck injury. The seizure episode cost Wolfe the rest of the season.

He did later join the Broncos in New Jersey for Super Bowl week and the expectation is he'll be ready for the 2014 season.

But this was the third defensive starter in three weeks the Broncos lost to a season-ending physical setback. More key defensive starters would follow.

The Broncos made it to Arrowhead Stadium and were standing at attention for the National Anthem when CBS cameras caught crocodile-sized tears streaming down Moreno's face.

"The emotion always gets to me," Moreno told reporters after the game. "I am just thinking about everything in general through your whole life, just balled up into one. Yeah, it helps me. Sometimes I don't even notice it, it just comes."

The stars of the game were Decker, who abused Chiefs cornerback Marcus Cooper and Brandon Flowers (among others) for four touchdown receptions, and rookie Montee Ball, who busted out for 117 yards on just 13 carries.

A second-round draft pick out of Wisconsin, where he broke all the NCAA career rushing records, Ball was selected by the Broncos ahead of Alabama's Eddie Lacy.

The Broncos thought Lacy had greater NFL potential, but they were concerned by the plate and screws that fused his big toe together.

"It was a close call," said John Elway. "It came down to the medical (report)."

The Pittsburgh Steelers also backed off Lacy because of his toe. Ball, the No. 58 overall pick, rushed for 559 yards and 4 touchdowns off 120 carries (4.7 yards per carry) in his rookie season. Lacy, taken No. 61 overall by Green Bay, was the NFL's Offensive Rookie of the Year after gaining 1,178 yards and 11 touchdowns on 284 carries (4.1 yards per carry).

Lacy clearly had the better rookie year. But the Broncos didn't take him because of durability concerns. We'll see.

Ball wound up on the better team. This win virtually clinched the Broncos' third AFC West title in three years. The Broncos improved to 10-2 after sweeping the two-game series from the Chiefs, who fell to 9-3.

By owning the head-to-head tiebreaker, the Broncos essentially had a two-game lead in the AFC West with four games left.

After the win, Elway presented the game ball to Jack Del Rio, who finished his interim term with a 3-1 record. It was known during the week that John Fox would return the Monday after this Chiefs' game.

"It was special to have John Elway recognize the things I did, but I basically want to say that it's just a representation of what we all did," Del Rio said. "It wasn't about me. It was a collective effort."

Said Manning, "Our team has faced a lot of adversity in just a short time. You never expect your head coach not to be with you the entire time. But Coach Del Rio has done a great job keeping us together. It was a pretty tough four-game stretch he had to endure, and the team responded. But we are certainly glad to have Coach Fox back."

Game 13 (11-2)	**Broncos 51** **Titans 28**	Sunday, Dec. 8 Denver, CO
Manning Stats	39 of 59 397 yards	4 TDs, 0 INTs
Breakout Player	Matt Prater K	
Key Injury	Wes Welker SR	

On the coldest day of the season – 18 degrees at kickoff – the smallest Denver crowd of the season – more than 5,600 no-shows – watched Manning emphatically school his cold-weather critics and Matt Prater boot his way past a 43-year-old record.

The theme of the week was Manning's struggles when the temperature was below 40 degrees and when the temperature was below 32 degrees. There were disparaging stats for both.

Doesn't every quarterback throw less effectively on cold days than warm?

"I've only been around him two years, but the thing that probably (ticks) me off more than anything is the fact that I don't want anybody else as my quarterback," Broncos offensive coordinator Adam Gase said Thursday prior to this game. "I'm going to go in with him every Sunday, and it's a great feeling to have. When you don't have a guy like that – and I've been in that spot a lot – it stinks when you know you walk in there and you don't have a shot. So I'll take him any day of the week."

The cold-weather shots seemed to calcify a chip on Manning's shoulder. He came out firing, throwing a short touchdown pass to Wes Welker to finish off his first drive. Welker would later suffer his second concussion in three weeks, forcing him to miss the final three games of the season.

But the Broncos as a group were flat for this one. They gave up a 57-yard pass to Titans' rookie receiver Justin Hunter on their first defensive series, followed by a 95-yard kickoff return to veteran Leon Washington, and then running back Shonn Greene scored on a ridiculously easy 28-yard run for a 21-10 lead.

The game changed, though, when Denver's defense came up with a three-and-out with 52 seconds left in the half.

It was 14 degrees as the seconds to the first half ticked down, when Manning completed a 7-yard pass to tight end Jacob Tamme with 3 seconds remaining.

The ball was on the Titans' 46. Perfect. When Prater saw holder Britton Colquitt put his hand down on the Broncos' 46 yard line, that's when he knew. All kickers know the NFL record field goal was 63 yards. All kickers know their 46-yard line is the magic mark for the record – 54 yards to the far goal line, another 10 yards through the end zone and over the goal posts.

Tom Dempsey, born with half a right foot, used a square-toed kicking shoe to kick a 63-yard field goal in 1970. His record had been tied by the Broncos' Jason Elam, Oakland's Sebastian Janikowski, and San Francisco's David Akers.

Elam and Janikowski kicked their record-tying field goals in Denver. Some people may want to discount Prater's record kick because of Denver's mile-high altitude.

"I think the cold took away whatever altitude helped," Prater said.

Aaron Brewer snapped the ball 8 yards back to Colquitt. Prater swung through and drilled a low liner that crossed the ball by maybe 18 inches. Good.

A 64-yard field goal and new record. Pandemonium at Sports Authority Field. The Broncos rushed out to swarm Prater. They were still down 21-20 as they went into the halftime break. But it felt like they were up 51-28.

Which they were by the time Manning lit up the Titans in the bitter cold second half.

"Whoever wrote that narrative can shove it where the sun don't shine," Manning told the Broncos' flagship radio station, 850 KOA in his postgame interview.

Game 14 (11-3)	**Chargers 27** **Broncos 20**	Thursday, Dec 12 Denver, CO
Manning Stats	27 of 41 289 yards	2 TDs, 1 INTs
Breakout Player	Andre 'Bubba' Caldwell WR	
Key Injury	Kayvon Webster CB	

This was the sixth primetime game the Broncos had played through their first 14 games. And they were in no mood for it. After the Broncos had thwacked Tennessee, Manning in his postgame press conference cracked wise about having to come back and play on Thursday.

"Terrible," said defensive tackle Terrance "Pot Roast" Knighton, when asked by *The Denver Post's* Joan Niesen about playing on Thursday night. "I say Thursday, I'm probably around 75 percent, 80 percent. By Saturday, I'm probably around 90, and Sunday morning I feel good."

The Broncos played like they didn't want to play. They got man-handled by a Chargers' team desperate to keep their playoff hopes alive.

The Chargers dominated both sides of the ball, again whipping the Broncos in time of possession, 39 minutes to 21. Broncos running backs Knowshon Moreno and Montee Ball combined for 18 yards on 11 carries – 1.6 yards per.

The Chargers, meanwhile, rushed for 177 yards on a staggering 44 carries.

Philip Rivers, perhaps the most hated player in Denver because of his trash-talking antics going back to Jay Cutler in 2007, only had to complete 12 of 20 passes for 166 yards for the decisive win. He did throw two touchdown passes to rookie Keenan Allen, who burned rookie corner Kayvon Webster on both plays. The Chargers were up 24-10 for most of the second half.

Webster suffered a broken thumb early in the game, played through it, but wound up with a cast and surgery the next day. Webster's play, and injury, meant veteran Champ Bailey could no longer rest his injured left foot. Ready or not, Bailey was returning to the Broncos' lineup.

The Chargers' defensive front had its way with the Broncos' offensive line and while Manning played respectably, the offense finished the first half with three consecutive, three-and-outs, totaling -1 yards.

The only other time the Broncos' offense had three consecutive drives without a first down was in the Super Bowl.

With Welker missing the first of three consecutive games because of his second concussion, Manning utilized No. 4 receiver Andre "Bubba" Caldwell, who led the team with six catches for 59 yards and two touchdowns.

Caldwell, though, was the only Bronco who showed up. Defensive coordinator Jack Del Rio had been experimenting with his secondary, benching strong safety Duke Ihenacho and giving second-year, converted cornerback Omar Bolden his first NFL start at free safety.

But after this game Del Rio made a commitment to veteran Mike Adams at free safety and Ihenacho at strong safety. As the Broncos tore off their pads following their listless defeat, Knighton called a defensive meeting in the losing locker room.

"I felt like it was the right time for it," Knighton said. "I said, 'If anything needs to be said, now's the time to let it on out.'"

This loss was a turning point for the Denver defense. Through 14 games, the Broncos ranked 26th in the 32-team NFL with an average of 26.6 points allowed. In their next four games—two in the regular season against Houston and Oakland and playoff victories over San Diego and New England – the Broncos allowed 15 points per game.

"We kind of made a pact after the San Diego loss – not taking anything away from San Diego, but we didn't have our best stuff," Fox said. "Basically, everybody made a pact that we're going to be the best we can be these last five games."

They were very good for four more. Not quite five.

Game 15 (12-3)	**Broncos 37** **Texans 13**	Sunday, Dec. 22 Houston, TX
Manning Stats	32 of 51 400 yards	4 TDs, 0 INTs
Breakout Player	Mike Adams S Eric Decker WR	Demarius Thomas WR Knowshon Moreno RB
Key Injury	Von Miller LB	

Peyton Manning was mobbed. Not by autograph seekers as he was leaving the stadium. By his teammates in the middle of the field after he had thrown his record-setting 51st touchdown pass with 4 minutes, 28 seconds remaining.

"It's never fun to be on the opposite end of a record-breaking performance," said Texans standout defensive lineman J.J. Watt, who got in a couple of licks on Manning.

Dressed immaculately in a suit and tie, Manning was standing in the sparse, cement-floored bowels of Reliant Stadium to accept another round of congratulations on his historic accomplishment.

It hardly seemed like the right place moments after one of the all-time greats delivered one of his unforgettable performances. Then again, the meager surroundings fit the perspective Manning gave to his latest passing record.

"The way the game is today, none of these offensive records will last," he said.

Manning entered this game with 47 touchdown passes, three shy of the single-season record New England's Tom Brady set in 2007. Manning put the Broncos up 10-3 when on the first play of the second quarter he connected with Demaryius Thomas on a 36-yard touchdown.

But entering the fourth quarter, Manning still had 48 touchdown passes as the Texans were surprisingly hanging tough, trailing 16-13.

The Texans edged the Atlanta Falcons as the NFL's most disappointing team in 2013. Through week 13 of the previous season, Houston had the AFC's best record at 11-1.

The Texans started this season 2-0. They would lose their final 14 games, a slump so horrific coach Gary Kubiak – a former longtime backup quarterback to John Elway and Broncos offensive coordinator until he took the Texans' top job after the 2005 season – was fired two weeks earlier.

Led now by interim coach Wade Phillips, the Texans gave the Broncos a game until the fourth quarter, when Houston's beleaguered veteran quarterback Matt Schaub was picked off by safety Mike Adams, who made a terrific play along the sidelines.

At that point Manning caught fire. He added TD pass No. 49 and the record-tying 50th to Decker in the fourth quarter, then set the record with a 25-yard touchdown pass to tight end Julius Thomas.

"I personally think all season records are going down, especially if they go to 18 games," Manning said. "And there won't be an asterisk next to them. Brady will probably break it again next year if not the year after."

A fan of the game long before he started dominating it, Manning held the TD pass record in higher regard than the yardage mark he was in position to break in the regular-season final at Oakland. "Touchdowns to me means it's helping your team win games," Manning said.

After this game against Houston, Manning had 5,211 yards – 266 shy of breaking Drew Brees' single-season record set two years earlier.

Decker and Demaryius Thomas combined for 18 receptions, 254 yards and 3 TDs against the Texans. Decker's two TDs gave him 10 for the season, boosting the Broncos' double-digit scorers to five, an all-time record.

Knowshon Moreno, who finished with 13 touchdowns, had another balanced game and surpassed the 1,000-yard milestone for the first time in his career. Moreno became the only Bronco running back in franchise history to have more than 1,000 yards rushing and 500 yards receiving in the same season.

Moreno's achievement was nearly overlooked. On the play after Moreno ran by 1,000, Manning passed for No. 49.

"It was definitely his moment," Moreno said. "He deserves it."

The 12th pick in the 2009 draft, Moreno was considered a disappointment through his first two seasons, when he rushed for only 947 and 779 yards. He suffered a knee injury in 2011 and was buried on the depth chart in 2012, when he was a healthy scratch for eight consecutive games.

He finished strong in 2012 but suffered another knee injury during the Broncos' playoff loss to Baltimore. After another knee surgery during the offseason, he ran third behind Ronnie Hillman and Montee Ball through early parts of training camp.

But after taking long looks at Hillman and Ball, Fox and running backs coach Eric Studesville felt the kids needed more time. Moreno was the starting tailback in the Broncos' season opener against Baltimore.

He has been the Broncos' top rusher ever since. Moreno's reward came Sunday in Houston where he became a 1,000-yard back.

"It's been a little journey, but every single bit of it has been lovely," he said. "It meant a lot with all the hard work I put in – not just me but the work the whole team put in. It was the first time in my career, so it was kind of special."

The win officially clinched the AFC West title and a first-round playoff bye.

But for all the records and accomplishments, the Broncos would suffer another dagger to their bid to win it all. On the first series, Von Miller's right knee buckled. He suffered a torn ACL that ended his nightmarish season.

"It's a blow," Fox said, "much like losing a guy like (offensive tackle) Ryan Clady earlier in the season. But our guys will deal with it."

They dealt with it until the final game. Clady and Miller were arguably the Broncos' second and third-best players.

Miller was easily the Broncos' most dominant defensive player in 2011 and 2012, registering 30 sacks in 31 games.

In March, he guaranteed via Twitter that the Broncos would win the Super Bowl. His year unraveled from there. In May, Miller learned there was an issue with one of his drug tests that eventually led to a six-game suspension for violating the NFL's substance-abuse policy.

In the midst of his suspension appeal, Miller was issued warrants for missing court appearances on speeding violations.

The Broncos went 6-0 during his absence, and upon his return he struggled to regain his all-pro form.

Miller had five sacks in the 10 games he played, well below the standard he set in his first two seasons. Still, it would have been better for the 115 million or so who watched the Super Bowl on Feb. 2 if the Broncos had Miller and Clady. And Derek Wolfe, Rahim Moore, Kevin Vickerson, and Chris Harris.

Game 16 (13-3)	**Broncos 34** **Raiders 14**	Sunday, Dec 29 Oakland, CA
Manning Stats	25 of 28 266 yards	4 TDs, 0 INT
Breakout Player	Brock Osweiler QB	Montee Ball RB
Key Injury	N/A	

Manning and his men only played a half. Which was a lot longer than Raiders' players, who seemingly left their cars running in the parking lot.

It's hard to believe Manning could play a more efficient half. He had his Broncos up 31-0 at halftime, then watched second-year backup Brock Osweiler run out the clock in the second half.

The win and the No. 1 playoff seed were assured. Manning needed 266 yards to break Drew Brees' record. Manning on his last pass, a 6-yard touchdown to Julius Thomas, gave him exactly 266 yards.

Manning finished the season with 55 touchdowns and 5,477 passing yards. Record and record.

The Broncos finished with 606 points. Record.

All that documentation presented a strong case Broncos fans had just witnessed the greatest offensive team, and the best single-season quarterback performance, in NFL history.

Next up was the single-elimination tournament that is the NFL postseason. The Broncos were heavy favorites to win the AFC championship.

"We got to stamp it," Decker said. "No question. This is like the first chapter of our season. It was big for us that we set ourselves up for success. Now we have to make sure we take care of business. This is when it really counts."

Given a bye which meant two weeks until their opening playoff game, Manning took a moment to reflect on his team's regular-season accomplishment.

"On the players' part, we have had a number of distractions, injuries, on the field situations, off-the-field situations," Manning said. "For the players, we've kept our focus on doing the players' jobs."

Yet, here they were with back-to-back 13-3s and back-to-back No. 1 seeds.

This season, though, wasn't about repeating 13-3. The Broncos just did that. Another 13-3 with an opening playoff loss would have meant a miserable season. The pressure was on for Manning and the Broncos to come through with at least one playoff win.

13: The Clouds Have a Silver Lining, the Sky is Predominantly Orange
MIKE KLIS

On the morning of Jan. 12, 2014, hours before the Broncos were to play their playoff opener against the San Diego Chargers, *The Denver Post* got the football world in a twitter.

The cover of the playoff special section was a full-page photo of Manning, hands behind his back holding the facemask of his helmet, looking off into an overcast distance.

An illustration of a dark cloud was overhead, superimposed by a large, white-faced headline that read:

A LEGACY
UNDER A CLOUD

Gulp. The accompanying story I wrote dealt with Manning's disappointing 9-11 playoff record that included eight, one-and-dones and just one Super Bowl title.

The edgy cover art drew enormous reaction across the country. At the very least, *The Denver Post* cover shot applied enormous pressure on Manning. At worst, the front page was an unfair buzzkill on the excitement of the Broncos' long-awaited 2013-season playoff opener.

Either way, the nation stirred.

ESPN reporter Sal Paolantonio held up the cover during his first Sunday morning report.

"Wow. Front of *Denver Post* playoff section," tweeted Stacey Dales of the NFL Network.

Melissa Stark re-tweeted her colleague with the notation, "That's just not right!"

Fox reporter Erin Andrews followed Stark's comment with, "At all."

Radio sports talk shows from San Diego to New York weighed in on *The Denver Post* cover.

If I may, this book on Jan. 12 should not have been judged by its cover. The story was far more sympathetic to Manning's postseason performances. It pointed out, from the opening sentence, how Manning did once drive off with a Cadillac Escalade as a Super Bowl MVP.

It also revealed how his stats during playoff defeat (29 TD passes vs. 14 interceptions) were considerably better than when Manning went 4-0 during his 2006-season playoff run with the Indianapolis Colts that ended with a ring (3 TD passes vs. 8 picks).

Still, there was no denying that in the subconscious of fans' minds, the perception of Manning's postseason record was harsher than reality.

One problem with Manning's postseason marks was the incredible standard he set during the regular season. His 167 wins are second only to Brett Favre's 186 but Manning has the better winning percentage.

But in the postseason, Manning's 9-11 record was worse than all but Dan Marino and Warren Moon among quarterbacks with at least 10 playoff starts. Marino and Moon are Hall of Famers but Manning has moved on to the conversation that considers the greatest quarterbacks of all time.

And this is where 9-11 is a long way from Joe Montana's 4-0 Super Bowl record.

As Manning was preparing to play his 21st career playoff game, second for the Broncos, against the Chargers at Sports Authority Field at Mile High, he was asked if he put too much pressure on himself to carry his team come playoff time.

"That's not how I feel," he said. "I guess everybody has a different theory or analysis."

With *The Denver Post*, I covered not only the Broncos but the NFL at large. This meant covering eight consecutive Super Bowls, from the end of the 2005 season through 2012, without the Broncos' participation.

In the week leading up to the Super Bowl that Manning won with the Indianapolis Colts in the 2006 season, he was often asked about the elusive Big Game.

"It seems like the definition of the Big Game is the one you lose," Manning said then. Now years later, during a one-on-one interview following a minicamp practice in June, 2013, I reminded Manning about his Big Game response.

"It seems not just with me but in many athletes' cases, if you win it becomes, 'Ah, well, you were supposed to win that,'" Manning said. "And then if you don't...

"I think every player will tell you they'd like to win every single game they played. I don't know if that's realistic in sports. You keep giving yourself opportunities. I like to be in the arena. I like to be in the mix. We were in the mix last year. We want to be back in it this year but we've still got a lot of work to do. This is a totally different season than last year but hopefully we give ourselves a chance."

The deflating manner in which the Broncos' 2012 season ended created a monstrous sense that even if they finished 15-1 in 2013

– or 13-3, as it turned out – but lost their first playoff game in the second round, then it was a bad season.

"That's football," Manning said. "Let's say you don't win the Super Bowl, don't go to the playoffs but you win that last game of the regular season. That locker room is kind of feeling good. 'Hey great win. Nice catch.' You're high fiving.

"But if you get in the playoffs, it's sudden death and... I'd rather be knocking on the door. I'd rather have your chance to win the game and go on knowing that if you lose it's going to be disappointing. But you want the opportunity.

"So the goal is to start with week one. To be an improving team throughout the regular season. In the NFL, it's so crazy you never know what team is going to – I get so tired of all this talk about strength of schedules. How do you have any idea what 2013 teams are going to be compared to 2012?"

Manning's peeve was prescient. The AFC West, considered weak beyond the Broncos in recent years, suddenly was the strongest in the conference. The Kansas City Chiefs, bolstered by new coach Andy Reid and quarterback Alex Smith, improved from the NFL's worst at 2-14 in 2012, to an 11-5 wild-card in 2013. The Chargers went from 7-9 and cleaning out its front office and coaching staff following the 2012 season, to 9-7 and winning a first-round playoff game on the road against the tough Cincinnati Bengals under their new regime of Tom Telesco (who made his mark with Manning's Colts) and Mike McCoy (who made his with Manning's Broncos).

In the playoffs' second round, the Chargers, winners of five consecutive games, would meet the Broncos.

The pressure was on Manning. And after blowing their second-round, home playoff game the previous year against Baltimore, the pressure was on the Broncos.

Manning methodically delivered. Conditions weren't ideal for passing at Sports Authority Field at Mile High – 41 degrees at kick-off with 17 mph winds. But Manning and the Denver defense took command from the jump.

As Jack Del Rio's defense forced Philip Rivers and the Chargers into punts on their two first quarter possessions, Manning led the Broncos on a 14-play, 86-yard drive on their first series. It took 7 minutes and 1 second – nearly half the quarter – and ended with a short Manning touchdown flip to Demaryius Thomas.

Early in the second quarter, after San Diego's Nick Novak missed a 53-yard field goal, the Broncos took advantage of good field position by ramming it down the Chargers' throats.

San Diego was the more physical team when they beat the Broncos in regular season, but it seemed a bit gassed coming off what was essentially five consecutive elimination game wins. A heavy dose of running backs Knowshon Moreno and Montee Ball put the ball on the 3-yard line where Manning on third down hit Wes Welker for the touchdown. The Broncos were up 14-0.

Welker was playing for the first time since a concussion forced him to miss the final three games of the regular season.

The Broncos missed a chance to bury the Chargers late in the first half when they had first-and-goal at the 4 with less than a minute remaining. On third down, Manning drilled a pass to the well-covered Eric Decker. The ball zinged through to Decker's pads but it bounced off and bounced high in the air. Chargers' linebacker Donald Butler caught it for a touchback.

It would be Manning's only blemish in the AFC playoff tournament.

The Broncos led 17-0 entering the fourth quarter, then held on after their best all-around cornerback, Chris Harris, went down with a torn ACL midway through the third quarter.

Philip Rivers brought a scare to Sports Authority Field by picking on his former teammate, and Harris' replacement, Quentin Jammer.

Rivers threw two touchdown passes to rookie Keenan Allen, who twice beat Jammer, and the Chargers had drawn to within 24-17 with 3:53 remaining.

Hold the Broncos on the next series and the Chargers would have been in position to pull off another disheartening comeback on the Broncos.

But Manning was clutch. He came through with two, third-down-converting completions to tight end Julius Thomas in the final minutes to ice it, including a third-and-17 while under pressure with 3:07 remaining.

"There were a lot of teams that had disappointing losses last year," said Manning, who finished 25-of-36 for 230 yards, two touchdowns, and an interception that bounced off his receiver's pads. "Atlanta and Washington and everybody said in that locker room let's get back next year – it just doesn't happen. It's hard to get back.

"I told the team (Saturday) night you need to be commended for getting back to this point. "It's hard to explain all the stuff we've been through all season. So to get to this point was really hard work and to win this game was a lot of hard work."

Up next for Manning and the Broncos: Tom Brady and the New England Patriots in the AFC Championship Game. Never mind Manning-Brady XV. This would be Manning and Brady for the right to play in Super Bowl XLVIII.

Over the years, the prevailing feeling was Manning was the more dominant quarterback but Brady was tougher when times got tough. Head-to-head, Brady was 10-4 lifetime against Manning.

Then again, Brady always had coach Bill Belichick on his side.

The AFC Championship Game was the Broncos' first since they were thumped at home by the Pittsburgh Steelers, 34-17 following the 2005 season.

In this conference championship, the temperature at Sports Authority Field was a made-for-Peyton 63 degrees.

Surprisingly, the game wasn't close.

Neither Brady nor Manning could get much going in the first quarter, although the Broncos' Matt Prater did kick the first of his four field goals. Early in the second quarter, the Broncos called a pick, or rub, play in which Welker crossing right to left collided with New England's best cornerback Aqib Talib, who was coming from the other direction while tracking receiver Demaryius Thomas.

Talib was knocked out of the game with a rib and ankle injury. The day after this game, Belichick said the play was intentional on Welker's part and it was the biggest play of the game. The NFL disagreed with the Patriots' ever-sore loser coach. After reviewing the play, the league determined it was a legal play. Welker was neither flagged during the game nor fined postgame.

Apparently, Talib had no problem with the play either. He signed a six–year, $57 million contract with the Broncos in March of 2014. Asked about the Welker hit, Talib said, "Wes is a good friend of mine. I watched that play 1,000 times and I can promise you he didn't do it on purpose."

The Broncos continued on for a 15-play, 94-yard drive that again lasted for 7 minutes and 1 second. Manning capped it with a 1-yard pass to backup tight end Jacob Tamme, who posted up a couple yards into the end zone.

It was 13-3 at halftime but on the opening possession of the third quarter, Manning again methodically moved the Broncos 90 yards on 14 plays, taking up 7 minutes, 8 seconds. His 3-yard touchdown pass to Demaryius Thomas made it, 20-3.

It became 23-3 with 12 minutes remaining when Brady smartly led two touchdown drives against a prevent-type Denver defense. Brady never quits, but it would be Manning going on to the Super

Bowl for the third time in eight years. It was the seventh Super Bowl for the Broncos, starting with the 1977 season.

The Broncos not only beat the Patriots, they beat back the demons from last year's horrific playoff loss to Baltimore.

"If we had to lose that game, I'm happy the way we lost," said Broncos right tackle Orlando Franklin. "It definitely made us a stronger team this year. It made us refocus."

Manning, meanwhile, continued to beat back his stubborn critics who insisted Brady was better in the clutch. In this game, Brady misfired on several big throws and Manning finished 32-of-43 for 400 yards, two touchdowns and no interceptions. To a man, his teammates were happy for him. They understood that only Manning has been criticized for not winning enough in the playoffs. And only Manning was individually ripped for not beating Brady enough.

"I'm definitely happy for that guy," Franklin said, nodding to his quarterback as Manning stepped gingerly to the showers. "He silenced a lot of critics today. I don't know if there's any person that works harder than he does."

Softened by the relief of victory, Manning was openly reflective on the postseason criticism he has received.

"Playing quarterback, there's certainly a number of things that come along with it," Peyton said. "You have to try to keep level-headed after a win, after a loss. You can't get too high or too low. That advice has served me well. I'm glad my teammates were happy for me – I'm happy for them. This truly has been a team this year.

"You have to eventually focus on doing your job when you're playing quarterback. That's what I was focused on today. Nothing more than that."

Manning was one step from capping the greatest quarterback season since the league was formed in 1920. In its 94th season, the league now had a QB who had thrown for 59 touchdowns and 6,107 yards while compiling a 15-3 record that included two clutch victories when it counted most, against the red-hot Chargers and mighty Patriots.

Manning engineered two touchdown drives in the AFC championship that took up more than seven minutes of game clock each. Those drives lasted a combined 28 plays, traveled a combined 173 yards and were finished by short Manning touchdown passes.

It was on to MetLife Stadium – home of the New York Giants and Peyton's younger brother, Eli – against the Seahawks.

It was all lining up to be Peyton's greatest season.

Instead, that dark cloud reappeared.

14: Bowlen's Broncos
WOODY PAIGE

There was a little more spring in Pat Bowlen's step as he passed through the Broncos' locker room after his team's 26-16 victory over the Patriots in the AFC Championship.

"Congratulations, Mr. B.," linebacker Wesley Woodyard said.

"Thanks to you players," Bowlen said.

Three other players reached out to shake his hand and the security guards accompanying Bowlen tried to hurry him along.

But Bowlen slowed, stopped, and stared at the joyous celebration for a moment, the lines in his thin face creased as he smiled.

Bowlen was returning to the Super Bowl for the first time in 15 years, and for the sixth time in his 30-year ownership of the Denver Broncos' franchise.

Uniquely, the only other current owner in the NFL who has guided his franchise to six Super Bowls was just down the hall at the stadium in Denver. Robert Kraft, owner of the Patriots, had the achievement to himself until Jan. 19, 2014.

Super Bowlen was back.

A couple of months earlier, in San Diego, Bowlen had reached another milestone – the 300th victory during his 30 season reign as owner of the Broncos. No other owner in the history of pro football had accumulated 300 in 30. His team's winning percentage of 60 during that span from 1984-2013 was second only to Tim Mara, owner of the Giants.

Not bad for a fellow who had failed to make it as a football player at the University of Oklahoma. Bowlen sure made it in the NFL. His team had gone to the Super Bowl at the end of the 1986, '87, '89, '97, '98 and, now, 2013. He owned back-to-back championships in '97-'98, and always will be remembered for holding the Vince Lombardi Trophy in San Diego after Super Bowl XXXII and shouting, "This one's for John."

The night before Elway was officially named as executive vice president of football operations (in January, 2011) he told me on the phone, "My No. 1 goal is to stand up on the podium after a Super Bowl and say 'This one's for Pat.'"

The football operation is now overseen by Elway, and the franchise is presided over by Bowlen's old friend and long-time Broncos' executive, Joe Ellis.

Since Ellis has stepped up, Bowlen has noticeably taken a back seat, and was notably missing at the Orlando owners meeting in March 2014. Mike Klis spoke to Ellis from Orlando for a fantastic article in *The Denver Post*, and Ellis said "Mr. Bowlen is at home in Hawaii. He's relaxing with his family. He's obviously taken a step back in the last few seasons. But he has set in stone a culture of winning that is understood by all of us with the Denver Broncos.

"He does have some health issues at this point in his life, but he's doing OK. Those are personal to him and personal to his family. He pushes through valiantly. The best news is, outside of this brief stay in Hawaii, he's around every day and enjoys going to practices and being around his football team."

Ellis and Elway, the E-Team, are trying to get Bowlen another Super Bowl victory.

In May of 2009, Pat and I had a long one-to-one (he normally has someone at his side when he talks to media) conversation on the phone, and I asked him about his health. "My health is good, but I have some short-term memory loss, like a lot of men at my age." It was a rather shocking admission.

I replied to him, "I sometimes walk into the kitchen, where I'm standing now, and I forget why I came in here. I understand." Bowlen is only three years older than I am.

"But I've forgotten things about the Super Bowls," Pat confessed.

That interview led to a lot of speculation about Bowlen over the past several years. He still goes into the office every day and works out in the Broncos' training center. Both Ellis and Elway report to Bowlen daily and he signs on every major decision the franchise makes. But, for most of the time during those 30 years, Bowlen was hands-on, and was involved in major and minor details. Not so much anymore. Bowlen once told me he would never sell the team. "I'll be here until they put me in a box." There are no indications these days that he will sell his ownership, and he does have a wife and five children, but he could bring in Elway as a minority partner. The two had discussed such a possibility when Elway was hired as executive V.P.

The franchise Bowlen purchased from Edgar Kaiser Jr. for just under $70 million (he didn't have 100 percent ownership until a year later) was valued, according to Forbes Magazine, in 2013 at $1.05 billion. That number will continue to rise, especially after another trip to the Super Bowl.

The man born to a Canadian wildcatter and a Wisconsin mother during World War II has done OK.

Bowlen told me years ago that his late father Paul D. Bowlen (for whom the Broncos' headquarters are named) and late mother Arvella (who spent the last several years of her life living in Denver) were traveling in a car through Vermillon, Canada, when she became ready to give birth. She chose to go back to her childhood home in Prairie du Chien, Wis., (population 6,000) and have their son, Dennis Patrick Bowlen.

He was a Can-Am Kid.

Paul, a mining and oil speculator, did extremely well with his drilling and became wealthy and, as a teenager, "Pat" was sent to the prestigious all-boys Catholic Campion High School. There, he was good but not great academically, and good but not great in hockey, football and track. He graduated in 1962 and went off to Oklahoma University.

As a freshman Pat spent some time with the powerful Sooners, coached by the legendary Bud Wilkinson, but quickly realized he was too small, too slow, and too average to be a college football player, and gave up the game.

Instead, Bowlen would earn degrees in business and law, and returned to Canada (Edmonton) to be a lawyer and an executive in his father's company. He made his mark and multiple millions in oil, gas and real estate investments. In his late 30s, Pat decided he wanted to "do something different and have some fun in life" and got into sports management – as an owner. He investigated hockey and Canadian Football League franchises. One day at church, Pat told me, he ran into fellow Canadian Edgar Kaiser Jr., who had recently bought the NFL's Denver Broncos and told him, "If you ever want to sell, let me be first in line."

When Kaiser started bleeding financially – and the Broncos, although few knew, were in danger of bankruptcy, he called Bowlen in 1984. Kaiser told me, "It was a simple transaction. I told Pat how much I wanted (more than doubling his outlay), he said yes. One of the easiest business deals I ever made."

Bowlen, who nobody in Denver had ever heard of, was introduced as the new Broncos owner on March 23, 1984. He said he would move to Denver, take command of the team personally, and return a championship to the city. "I'm not here to play around. I'm here to win," Pat told me then.

Then he showed up on the sideline at a game in a flamboyant fur coat.

That was not the right thing to do. "I made a mistake," he acknowledged later. But Bowlen liked the spotlight. He purchased a mansion next to the famed Cherry Hills Country Club (to go with his Oceanside home beneath Diamond Head and outside Honolulu, Hawaii) and regularly attended charity events. He was at every Broncos practice, ordered a luxury suite renovated above the 50-yard line at Mile High Stadium for his pleasure at games and then trained for, and finished 135th (among more than 1,000 entries) in the grueling Ironman Triathlon on the Big Island of Hawaii.

Bowlen was in the best shape of any owner in the league and he helped the other owners get into better shape as the head of the broadcasting committee. Bowlen negotiated an $18 billion contract with the networks to televise NFL games.

Meanwhile, the Broncos started going to Super Bowls shortly after Bowlen took over – because of the presence of John Elway – and became one of the most successful teams in football. When Bowlen brought back former assistant Mike Shanahan to take over as coach (and everything else in the front office) and opened up his pocketbook for free agents and free spending, the Broncos ultimately won two Super Bowls.

However, hard times were ahead after Elway retired. The Broncos did make the 2005 AFC Championship, but generally were a .500 team for years. Bowlen had promised that Shanahan had a lifetime contract. But that life with the Broncos ended at the very beginning of 2010 when Shanahan was fired by Bowlen – and replaced with Kid McDaniels.

On the night Bowlen fired McDaniels, he and Elway celebrated at Elway's restaurant in Cherry Creek and the two agreed to hook up again. John Fox would be hired as coach, Tim Tebow would have a short, brilliant run (literally), and Peyton Manning would agree to join the Broncos' drive.

Bowlen's Broncos were back.

And Bowlen had become a serious candidate to one day be in the Pro Football Hall of Fame.

15: Lead Up to the Big Game

WOODY PAIGE

Like Jake and Elwood, aka the Blues Bros. (sounds like two old Denver quarterbacks), the Broncos were on a mission.

The journey was almost complete when they arrived at the Super Bowl.

One more game, one more victory, one more hurdle, and mission accomplished.

The heartbreak from the Broncos' devastating double-overtime playoff loss to Baltimore to finish the 2012 season could have sent the Denver franchise in one of two directions: they could have been deflated knowing that all their hard work while racking up 11 decisive victories to finish the 2012 regular season meant nothing in the end; or they could intensify their focus and dial up their motivation.

One of the star players on the 2007 Patriots, slot receiver Wes Welker, stunningly signed with the Broncos as a free agent prior to the 2013 season. Welker became the common denominator in the two most prolific offenses in NFL history.

Coincidentally, or maybe not, each of those high-powered offenses were shut down in their respective Super Bowls. The 2007 Patriots had averaged 36.8 points per game during the regular season but managed just 14 in an upset Super Bowl loss to the New York Giants.

The 2013 Broncos averaged 37.9 points per game during the regular season but scored 8 meaningless points against the terrific Seattle Seahawks.

There was no good place to introduce the Super Bowl calamity in the story of the Broncos' 2013 season. It might as well drop in as an interruption.

Where were we? Oh, yes, Welker. The combination of Manning having a second year of familiarity with Denver, the addition of Welker, All Pro right guard Louis Vasquez and tight end Julius Thomas, and a more explosive, fast-break pace catapulted the Broncos' offense to unprecedented heights.

The Broncos not only scored 37.9 points per game in 2013, they averaged 10.1 points better than the next-highest scoring team, the Chicago Bears.

The Broncos' averaged 457.3 yards per game – 40 more than the runner-up Philadelphia Eagles whose new coach, Chip Kelly, brought a turbo-powered college offense with him from Oregon.

Until 2013, no NFL team ever had more than three players score at least 10 touchdowns in a season. The 2013 Broncos had five: receiver Demaryius Thomas (14), running back Knowshon Moreno (13), tight end Julius Thomas (12), receiver Eric Decker (11) and the slot man Welker (10).

And until 2013, there had never been an NFL quarterback who put on a single-season performance like Peyton Williams Manning. Until this season, no quarterback had thrown more than the 50 touchdown passes New England's Tom Brady compiled in 2007. Until this season, no quarterback had accumulated more than the 5,476 passing yards that New Orleans' Drew Brees recorded in 2011.

Manning broke both marks with 55 touchdowns and 5,477 yards – sitting out the second half of the Broncos' final game rout at Oakland.

"What I think is amazing is, when I did it, I was 24," said Dan Marino, of the 5,084 passing yards he put up in 1984, a record that held for 27 years until Brees went by in 2011. "He's had four neck surgeries and missed a year and now he's 37 and doing what he's doing. It's pretty amazing what they're doing now, the Denver Broncos."

For the second consecutive season, the Broncos finished 13-3, tied for the NFL's best record, and No. 1 playoff seed in the AFC.

"It's not easy to go back-to-back 13-3s," said coach John Fox. "It's not easy to go back-to-back one seeds. Obviously, everybody in our building, our city, probably our region, maybe even the country, was disappointed how we finished a year ago. Hopefully that's been a fire in the belly since that last January."

The Broncos were 2 ½ point favorites to beat the Seahawks in the Super Bowl.

The Super Bowl's AFC representative – the designated "home" team (it alternates every year) – would wear its home uniforms. In this case, the Broncos would wear orange.

Happy, happy, right?

Well, the Broncos had never won a Super Bowl wearing orange jerseys. Their two victories in six appearances were in blue jerseys in Super Bowl XXXII against the Packers and white jerseys in Super Bowl XXXIII. The Broncos had switched in 1997 to dark blue, Nike-designed uniforms, although Pat Bowlen (who wasn't supposed to be color blind) claimed the team's color remained "predominantly orange" (there was orange piping on the jerseys and pants).

The Broncos returned to orange jerseys in 2011, even though John Elway wasn't thrilled about the idea. Elway loved the blue.

Just before his 50th birthday, John and I had a long conversation for a column and a front-page interview to commemorate the occasion at the popular steakhouse he co-owns in Denver's upscale Cherry Creek neighborhood.

With his blue jersey on display in a nearby case on the way, John made a point of saying: "You know, I never lost a game wearing blue." You're kidding.

"Think about it. We won all our home games in 1997 and 1998 in the blue jerseys, and we won the Super Bowl in blue (after playing on the road in the playoffs). My final season we also won the playoff games in blue. If you go back, I lost Super Bowls wearing orange."

The Broncos still wear blue as an alternative jersey for rare games, but would be in the usual orange against the Seattle Seahawks, who would be in white rather than their snappy blue-and-green jerseys.

Perhaps that was the first mistake for the Broncos.

The second was the cruise ship. For the first time in league history, a team conducted its Wednesday and Thursday media interviews on a cruise ship.

The Broncos' headquarters for game week was the Hyatt Regency in Jersey City, across the Hudson River from New York City. The Seahawks were staying about a mile away.

I actually thought it was a brilliant idea that the Broncos had leased the Cornucopia Majesty for team interviews and probably a post-game party. I suggested to Broncos president Joe Ellis that he and his staff had been very creative.

"We didn't do it. The NFL did because there wasn't enough ballroom space in the Hyatt for the interviews."

Nevertheless.

But some "brilliant" mind in the NFL office forgot one aspect.

The Broncos got seasick, even though the ship was tied to the dock on the cold waterfront. There was choppiness on the Hudson and swaying on the ship, and the players felt it.

Several had faces that were "predominantly blue."

Corner Quentin Jammer among them.

"I don't like the boat," he told Kevin Manahan of NJ.com as his head (Jammer's, not Manahan's) rested on the table. "I'm not feeling very good with all this rocking. I don't know who thought to have these interviews on the boat, but it's really not a good idea."

Alfred Williams, a defensive end on the Broncos' 1990s Super Bowl teams, currently is a radio talk show host in Denver. After a few minutes on the ship, Williams bolted, citing seasickness.

Spoiler alert: When the Broncos were blown out by the Seahawks in the Super Bowl, they didn't blame the ship. But the gigantic, bold headline on the front page of *The Denver Post* the following morning blared one word:

SEASICK

Backup defensive tackle Sione Fua had said on Thursday during the mass interview session, "I have a headache from all the rocking. Yesterday was worse. Why couldn't we do this in the hotel? It makes no sense. If they didn't have a big enough ballroom, we could have done it in the hallway."

The Seahawks would be doing their interviews in a ballroom that did not rock or roll.

Dominique Rodgers-Cromartie said he felt queasy. "This is my first time really being on a boat, but I still want to take a cruise."

The old rock standard "Sea Cruise" was not played in the locker room, and the Broncos did not show the players the new Robert Redford movie *All Is Lost*, about a sailor trapped alone on the ocean.

ALL IS LOST

That would have been a good headline for the Broncos' Super Bowl story, too.

Defensive back David Bruton said he suffers from motion sickness. "I don't like the water. I've seen *Titanic*."

Speaking of disasters, there's another headline possibility:

BRONCOS GO DOWN LIKE TITANIC

Where was Molly Brown, who saved so many people on the Titanic, when the Broncos needed her? She lived in Denver – her house is a favorite tourist attraction.

The Broncos might as well have spent most of the first half rearranging the deck chairs.

The ship wasn't the Broncos' only problem during the week in New Jersey. Not only did the Seahawks get the nicer hotel, but they practiced daily at the Giants' facility next to MetLife Stadium. The Broncos were stuck with the Jets' training center at Florham Park, N.J.

John Fox moved the team's Thursday practice indoors, not because of the weather, but because of the risk of injury outside on the frozen synthetic turf. "We just came inside because it (the turf) was softer. It was more for the players' legs than anything else. The field got a little hard yesterday." Fox did order that the doors be left open so the Broncos could get a feel of the Arctic conditions (wind chill of 18 degrees).

Despite the hard turf and shaking ship, the Broncos seemed to be having good, solid workouts during the week. The gameplans for the offense and the defense had been installed back in Denver the previous week, and Fox had put together a plan based on his two previous trips to the Super Bowl. Both were losses, though, when he was the defensive coordinator with the New York Giants for Super Bowl XXXV (2001) and as the head coach of the Carolina Panthers for XXXVIII (2004). The first was a blowout victory by Baltimore (34-7), but the Panthers were almost up against the New England Patriots in Houston, barely losing 32-29.

The Broncos had only four players with Super Bowl experience. But the Seahawks had none.

With a victory in the game, Fox would earn a $1 million Powerball kind of bonus. As it was, Elway already had said Fox, who would be entering his final contract year in 2014, would be getting an extension and a raise.

Fox would make a pre-game mistake, however, by not preparing for a hostile environment at MetLife Stadium. The Broncos didn't crank up the noise at practices because Fox believed that the crowd would be neutral. In fact, most believed that the crowd might be more pro-Broncos because of Peyton Manning's popularity to those who didn't have a dog in the hunt. The Broncos had become America's Favorite Team, according to television ratings during the season and surveys taken about the NFL franchise. After all, Manning had produced the greatest single-season numbers in the history of football.

Fox's theory about the neutral crowd was erroneous, as the Broncos learned on the first offensive play of the game.

However, in Manhattan during the week, the Broncos' following was more on display. Walk around Times Square, and there was a scarcity of Seahawks jerseys and colors. Several bars in midtown offered themselves as "Broncos Headquarters," and souvenir salesmen said Broncos' gear was outselling Seahawks swag 2-to-1.

Seahawks fans were late-comers from the Great Northwest, or maybe they all had rooms in Hoboken or Secaucus.

Players from the two teams certainly weren't causing trouble, unlike at some previous Super Bowls. Nobody was arrested for trying to hire an undercover (no pun intended) cop posing as a hooker, and there were no reports of players showing up at the team hotels at 4 a.m., or dancing in clubs at 3 a.m., or presenting themselves at the ESPN or Maxim or Playboy parties.

In fact, I never saw rowdy or raucous fans of the two teams. In New Orleans at Super Bowls, there were always dust-ups among loyalists of the two teams, and players could be seen wandering Bourbon Street or hanging out in Pat O'Brien's early in the week.

It was more reminiscent of the Super Bowl in early February of 2006 in Detroit. The game was indoors at Ford Field, and virtually nobody was outdoors downtown. The Seahawks lost that one to the Steelers, 21-10. Between the Broncos and the Seahawks, there had been five previous defeats in The Big Game.

By Friday, the players were finished with the yacht and the interviews. The biggest happening for the NFL was the honors award night at Radio City Music Hall.

Meanwhile, the Broncos were on the other side of the Hudson River having their dinner. But not on a boat.

After the team dinner Friday night in the hotel ballroom, Manning arose and told the other players to push the tables and chairs against the wall.

Would there be dancing?

No.

To relax the team, Peyton grabbed a football and told the Broncos they were going to do a walk-through of the game's intended early plays.

Only thing was, the Broncos did not practice a safety...

16: Super Bowl XLVIII

WOODY PAIGE

AND MIKE KLIS

Paige: The beginning was ghastly, grisly, and gruesome. A safety on the first offensive play!

Klis: From the first snap, the Broncos were a disaster.

Paige: I don't know who was more nervous, Mike – Broncos center Manny Ramirez or you. Manny was not being Manny, or being kind of Manning, and when I turned to look at you in the pressbox before the game, you had just dropped your roast beef sandwich on the floor. First turnover of the game. That should have been an indicator.

Klis: I think it was turkey. I looked around the stadium and thought, Uh-oh. More green and blue than orange. Maybe this wouldn't be a neutral site after all.

Paige: Mike, just down the road between here and New York City is Weehawken, New Jersey. We didn't realize that it should be called Seahawken, N.J.

Klis: I remember, Woody, when we were driving from Boston up to Foxborough for the Broncos-Patriots regular-season game in late November, and it was about 500 below zero, and we were talking about how Manning and the Broncos didn't stand a chance that Sunday, and they got off to that 24-0 halftime lead, and we decided then and there, over a bowl of chow-duh, that nobody was going to beat the Broncos, and they were going to run away with the Super Bowl.

Paige: Shows you how much we know. My friend called me two nights before the Super Bowl from Las Vegas, and wanted to know if he should bet on the Broncos or the over-under in the game. The Broncos were favored by 2½, and the over-under was 47 ½. I told him I couldn't pick my mother out of a police lineup, but I'd take the Broncos and the over.

Klis: How did that work out for you?

Paige: Not me. Him. SPOILER ALERT for those who haven't heard what happened in the Super Bowl. My friend John told me he won money on the Broncos. How, I asked? He said he bet the over, and the Broncos gave up a touchdown in the fourth quarter, and he had the Seahawks scoring the first points in the game, and you know what happened on the first play of the game, Mike.

Klis: Good thing you got back from the bathroom just before that snap.

Paige: Before the game, Commissioner Roger Goodell stood on the field, looked around at the late-arriving fans and said to an official, "I think it will be a Broncos crowd." On the sideline, Broncos coach John Fox said to an assistant, "I think we have more (fans) than they do."

Klis: The commish and the coach would be wrong. Although, it's not like we ever got a chance to hear from Broncos fans. Collective groans don't move the meter.

Paige: Too bad the Super Bowl wasn't a snowout. Too bad it was a blowout.

Klis: Let there be no doubt, experience can be overrated.

Paige: Damon Runyon, one of my two writing idols, once wrote, "The race is not always to the swift, nor the battle to the strong, but that's the way to bet." Don't forget that, Mike. Strong, stronger than a rent check. Who has the stronger team in this Super Bowl? My other writing idol and friend, Dan Jenkins, told a whole story in one of his books about betting on football games, and the bookie told the ol' boys that there was nothing in this whole wide world that is "dead solid perfect." And you're right about experience not mattering. Consider the Buffalos Bills in their third and fourth consecutive Super Bowl appearances to finish their 1992 and '93 seasons.

Klis: Or see Greg Norman with a Sunday morning lead in a major.

Paige: Ouch! I was there when Norman threw up all over Augusta National in the fourth round. When I saw him buggy-jerk his tee shot on No. 16 into the pond, I thought, here's a guy who wants to instantaneously combust. He is not a nice guy. He had plenty of experience gagging.

Klis: The Seahawks didn't have one player on their active 53-man roster with Super Bowl experience. Their coach, Pete Carroll, had never been part of a Super Bowl team. The Broncos, meanwhile, had four players who had played on the big stage, including Peyton Manning. And two of their top four coaches – Fox and defensive coordinator Jack Del Rio – had prior Super Bowl experience.

Paige: Yes, Fox had 2 previous trips to the Super Bowl but both were losses. One when he was the defensive coordinator with the New York Giants for XXXV (2001) and the other as the head coach for the Panthers for XXXVIII (2004).

Klis: Fox's Panthers nearly upset the Patriots before falling 32-29. His Giants got ripped, 34-7, by the Ravens, who that season employed Del Rio as linebackers coach.

Paige: Small NFL world. And Fox and Del Rio would both be the head coaches of the Broncos in 2013. Did anybody wonder what would have happened if Fox had been told by doctors not to coach the rest of the year, and Del Rio was the head coach in the Super Bowl?

Klis: The experience worked against Fox. He thought it would be a neutral crowd so in the Broncos' first Super Bowl practice at the Jets' facility, he didn't put the speakers on full blast.

Paige: For those from another planet, Mike, the teams practice with screechingly loud noise over the speakers, to simulate crowd noise, so they know what it will sound like when they're playing.

Klis: Pete Carroll, for instance, had his Seahawks practice with a blend of James Brown soul and Notorious B.I.G. hip-hop, according to the pool report written up by Sports Illustrated's Peter King. Not necessarily because Carroll worried about crowd noise, but because the young-minded Carroll prefers loud music.

Paige: It made a difference. Although the Broncos and the Seahawks each received about 13,500 tickets, and the stadium attendance (82,529) appeared evenly divided, there was a 12th man the Broncos hadn't anticipated. According to those who analyzed the secondary ticket market, people from the state of Washington bought twice as many tickets as did those from Colorado.

Klis: That's right. Fox underestimated how Super Bowl crowds have changed in recent years. No longer are they of the corporate, wine-and-cheese variety. Starting with Super Bowl XL in Detroit when 95% of Ford Field was filled with Terrible Towel-waving Steeler fans, NFL crowds have figured out how to travel. Expense be damned.

Paige: The coin toss should have been a tipoff that the game would be odd. As referee Terry McAulay announced for the whole world to hear that Namath would do the traditional coin flip, the old quarterback reacted prematurely and tossed. McAulay caught the coin, though, before it hit the turf and laughingly handed it back to Namath. Rather than cover the coin as the referee usually does, Namath showed it to the Seahawks, who, as the "visiting" team would make the call. Heads was up. Seahawks linebacker and co-captain Heath Farwell called tails. The downside generally will land on the upside.

Klis: Tails landed up.

Paige: Thanks for the inside tip, Mike.

Klis: Just wanted to see if you were keeping up. I saw you go off to the lunch room in the pressbox at this point and get some meatballs.

Paige: Super Bowl makes a man hungry. At least I didn't drop 'em.

Klis: About that coin toss. It actually meant more to the Broncos than some might think.

Paige: More times than not over the course of the season, the Broncos started the game on defense – because they won the toss and chose to defer, or because the other team won the toss and elected to receive. It's an old Patriots ploy. You can look it up. Teams deferring always get the offense in the second half, and usually end the first half with the ball. And the Broncos, of 2013, scored a majority of the time at the end of the first half and the beginning of the second half.

Klis: But the Seahawks elected to defer. Seattle coach Pete Carroll said, "We got what we wanted." For the Seahawks, defense is their strength. They love to start the game by having their physical defense set the tone.

Paige: After a poor kickoff return by Trindon Holliday, the Broncos would open at their own 14. Peyton Manning lined up in the shotgun, and the Broncos shot themselves in the feet.

Klis: Despite all the hype regarding Manning's legacy, despite all the analysis that poured over this supposedly intriguing match-up between the NFL's No. 1 offense and No. 1 defense, this Super Bowl was decided on the first snap.

Paige: And crowd noise caused the Broncos to botch that first snap!

Klis: We're coming full circle here. Manning realized his offensive linemen could not hear him. He stepped up toward the line and was going to tell everyone when to go.

Paige: Just as he has more than a thousand times during the season before the Super Bowl, Manning looked over the defense, then made a move toward the line to prepare to shout orders to the offense.

Klis: As Manning stepped up, center Manny Ramirez snapped the ball, over Manning's right shoulder and into the end zone. What da?!

Paige: Might as well have snapped it into deep space. Or onto the New Jersey Turnpike and into the Vince Lombardi rest stop. The Super Bowl trophy and a rest stop in New Jersey are named in honor of the late Packers coach. Of course, when his team won the first two NFL-AFL championship games, it wasn't the Super Bowl, and there was no trophy honoring Lombardi. Or a rest stop. Catch us up, Mike.

Klis: "It was real loud," Ramirez said. "None of us heard the snap count. I thought I did and…"

Paige: Most of the Broncos had no clue what was taking place behind them. Running back Knowshon Moreno did, though. He started chasing the bouncing ball into the end zone and, fortunately, recovered it before the Seahawks could.

Klis: But his hustle could not prevent the safety. Just 12 seconds in, the Seahawks had the fastest score in Super Bowl history.

Paige: Fox said, "It was a little louder than we thought." Oh, really, coach?

Klis: In fairness to Fox, the Broncos had been practicing with crowd noise all season. From the week of their first preseason game at San Francisco to their final road game at Oakland, crowd noise blared from several speakers during the Broncos' practices. Even if Fox turned down the volume during Super Bowl week, a Broncos offense led by Manning – who has been accused of being over-prepared – should have handled the opening snap. Crowd noise or no crowd noise.

Paige: The crowd, the score and the momentum were on Seattle's side, and the game began cascading away from the Broncos. Mike, you were sitting two seats away and I remember saying to you, "This doesn't feel right. I've seen too many of these."

Klis: Good gut, Woody. The game lasted 3 hours and 23 minutes – quick by Super Bowl standards as both teams mercifully ran the clock in the fourth quarter – but long enough to turn the Broncos from the toast of the NFL to a national punch line.

Paige: We've seen this four times before. Orange crushed again. This one's the most excruciating, though. The difference between the others and No. 48 was that the "most prolific offense" in NFL history played like the "most offensive team" in Super Bowl history.

Klis: The Seahawks did nothing to deserve their early lead – other than bring along their 12th Man. From that first play, the Broncos became unglued. They fell behind 8-0 by the end of the first quarter, 22-0 at halftime, and 29-0 after Percy Harvin finished off his 87-yard kickoff return just 12 seconds into the second half.

Paige: The fight should have been called off, mercifully, then and there.

Klis: In both halfs, the Seahawks scored 12 seconds in – on plays while their offense watched from the sideline. Pathetic. Inexcusable. Did they not practice after beating New England? The Broncos were destroyed, 43-8.

Paige: Demaryius Thomas said the Broncos "came out ready to play." The Broncos acted like they had never played, or even practiced. They fumbled, bumbled, and crumbled.

Klis: The Seahawks utterly dominated. In particular, their defense bullied the Broncos' offense. Not that Denver's defense did much better. The four missed tackles during Jermaine Kearse's 23-yard catch-and-twirl-and-touchdown to put Seattle up 36-0 were inexcusable.

Paige: Fox said there were "a couple of plays we didn't execute as well as they did." How about 125 plays?

Klis: This game was supposed to crown Manning's legacy, capping the greatest individual performance by a quarterback in NFL history. Instead, criticism that Manning is not the same in the big games resurfaced. His two first-half interceptions led directly (pick six) and indirectly to 14 Seattle points. The snap snafu gave Seattle two more.

Paige: Peyton Manning broke the Super Bowl record for pass completions (34). A hollow record. Peyton won everything this year but the one thing he wanted. He played terrible. Yet, afterward, when asked if it was embarrassing, Peyton said no. He might want to re-think that answer.

Klis: He rushed his first throw, trying to make a play on 3rd and long. Very bad throw. Started the avalanche. Second pick was go-ing to be a touchdown– Demaryius Thomas had Richard Sherman whipped on a post pattern and safety Earl Thomas III was late get-ting back. But Cliff Avril blew up right tackle Orlando Franklin on the play. Manning was clobbered. Pick six. Ball game. Thanks for the worthless two weeks of hype.

Paige: "Peyton didn't play that bad," his supporters claim. Yes he did. Peyton played his worst game since joining the Broncos. He was never ever in control. When the score was 22-0 at halftime I wrote this note to myself, "In six quarters at MetLife Stadium the Seahawks have held the Manning Bros. to 0 points." It ended up being eight. The Giants had been defeated 23-0 at this stadium late in the regular season. But, then, Eli had an awful season. Certainly, a lot more was expected from Peyton.

Klis: The defense couldn't get off the field on third down. And special teams were brutally bad.

Paige: Actually, the Broncos' defense – although being dominated on the field – held up its end on the scoreboard for quite a while into the third quarter. But the defense and the dam broke. The Broncos' defensive line never sacked or touched Russell Wilson, and when some pressure was applied, Wilson escaped. Robert Ayers took too many inside routes allowing Wilson, and Percy Harvin twice, to go for big gains. Blown coverages, missed tackles (sixth on touchdown run), poor recognition, and awful effort. The offensive, defensive, and special teams' game plans must have been written in crayon. Fox and his staff obviously were out-coached, and the Broncos were out-played.

Klis: What about the running game?

Paige: What running game – 27 yards on 14 carries? Receivers dropped balls and pulled up routes or couldn't escape. Total team mess. Until the final play of the third quarter, the Broncos had not scored, but had given up a safety, two field goals, a running touchdown, a passing touchdown, an interception touchdown, and a kickoff return touchdown. Finally, the Seahawks gave up a meaningless touchdown at quarter's end.

Klis: Hillary Clinton tweeted late in the Super Bowl, "It's so much more fun to watch Fox when it's someone else being blitzed & sacked!" One of the most humorless politicians of the past 50 years cracked funny at the Broncos' expense.

Paige: That wasn't as bad as Jay Leno, in his Monday monologue for *The Tonight Show*. He opened with 90 seconds of Bronco-bashing material.

"Was that the worst Super Bowl ever? The Puppy Bowl was more competitive. ...

"A lot of Broncos fans are sick over this. In fact, in Denver, fans went from smoking recreational marijuana to medical marijuana. ...

"The last time I saw a Bronco going that slow, OJ was driving it through L.A. ...

"In fact the team was so ineffective today they were invited to join the Obama administration."

No wonder Leno gave up his show. Those slow, white Bronco jokes were around when Elway was playing. Puppy Bowl? I guess, though, if you lose like that, you deserve what you get. I know I wrote before the game the 48 reasons the Broncos would win. Trust me. I've heard from about 48,000 emailers from Seattle telling me I was wrong. D'oh.

Klis: To make matters worse, the Seahawks couldn't stop insulting the Broncos in the days after the game. Star cornerback Richard Sherman popped off incessantly, saying the Super Bowl was really the NFC championship game between his Seahawks and San Francisco 49ers.

Paige: Sherman also claimed his Seahawk secondary picked up on Manning's hand audibles in the first half. They "jumped" routes, knowing where receivers would go and where Manning would throw. The Broncos didn't adjust. The Broncos didn't uncover any Seahawks secrets.

Klis: Pete Carroll bragged on the radio, "We really felt like we could knock the crud out of those guys."

Paige: Crud? For Pete's sake!

Klis: You know, Woody, there should have been more evidence from the preseason game between these teams. Even though the starters didn't play that long, Seattle ripped the Broncos 40-10. That's 88-17 in two thumpings. ESPN.com had a headline before the Super Bowl that begged the question, "Does the preseason matchup matter?" I think we all know the answer. The teams do play again in 2014. Twice. They open the preseason in August and then they'll meet again in the regular season in Seattle. Ugh. Just what the nation wanted.

Paige: Linebacker K.J. Wright said he thought the Seahawks could beat the Broncos "90 times out of 100." Wright is wrong. These Broncos would lose all 100.

Klis: But look at it this way: if the Seahawks played the Super Bowl without left tackle Russell Okung, cornerback and best defensive player Richard Sherman, safety Earl Thomas, defensive end/tackle Michael Bennett, defensive ends Cliff Avril and Chris Clemons, and center Max Unger, would they have beat the Broncos?

Paige: That's essentially what the Broncos had to do; they played without left tackle Ryan Clady, top defensive back Chris Harris, safety Rahim Moore, best pass rusher Von Miller, defensive end/tackle Derek Wolfe, defensive tackle Kevin Vickerson, and center Dan Koppen/J.D. Walton. *That's 9 starters of 22.* The Broncos' depth was dicey when guys were picked off the street and the practice squad.

Klis: Come on, Seattle. You beat up Peyton Manning and a bunch of "B" teamers.

Paige: Seattle was near perfect in anticipation and changing coverages to confound Peyton. The Seahawks effectively blanked Julius Thomas with a linebacker and generally played one-deep safety and had seven defenders on five receivers. The one deep pass from Manning to Demaryius Thomas was open, but overthrown. Manning was held to 4 of 11 on passes of 10-plus yards.

Klis: After his press conference, Manning climbed down from the podium and walked right by me. I was going to ask him a question or two, but he stuck his hand out to me, shook my hand and said, "Mike, sorry man." I was disarmed. I couldn't ask a question after that. I think Peyton knew I spent the year chronicling history and then in the end, history was not made.

Paige: Nobody from the Broncos apologized to me.

Klis: Maybe because they knew what you were going to write.

Paige: Super Bowl XLVIII was over way before it was officially over. It was over when Percy Harvin returned the woefully short second half kickoff for a touchdown. At that point, I began to think about what the lede of my column would be. For one of the few times in my 50 years of writing columns, the opening sentence came to me instantly.

Klis: I know I read it but why don't you refresh my memory.

Paige: You're kidding me, Mike. You know I wrote about Pat Bowlen saying after the Broncos finally won a Super Bowl, "This one's for John." So this time I wrote, *"This one's for the john."*

Klis: Print it.

Paige: Say good night, Mike.

Klis: Good night, Weehawken and Seahawken.

17: Where Do They Go From Here?
MIKE KLIS

Two days after the Massacre at MetLife Stadium, Elway and Fox held a joint, season-ending press conference at Broncos' headquarters. The line of questioning focused mostly on the 43-8, final-game debacle than the 15-3, record-setting accomplishment that delivered the Broncos to the Big Game.

Fox answered the final question. The press conference was adjourned.

"And I want to say one thing," John Elway said.

The press conference was not yet finished. Elway had the floor.

"And I want to say one thing. I kind of get the sense that these questions are, 'How the hell are we going to overcome this?' Right? The bottom line is, sure, it's not even 48 hours away from the game. But I will tell you this: Right now the focus is on what happened, instead of how we got there, and what we did this year and what we went through as a team.

"And I say that the farther you get away from this, the less you concentrate on just that one game, the more you look at the full season and really what we did as a football team and as an organization. And I tell you what, I'm very proud of that.

"There are some changes we've got to make and we'll make those. But the thing is, we can use that as a game that, OK, we now know what it's like to be there, now we're going to use that as the experience of we've been there but we've got to start with step one again and start with the offseason program.

"And April 21 – everybody that knows it comes in here and the people that we bring in here when it gets to 85-90 guys on the roster, John (Fox) readdresses this team the first time and again it's to get back and be world champions.

"The goal has not changed and it will not change. We will use this as an experience that we went through, be disappointed that we didn't play better, but the bottom line is this organization and what Pat Bowlen wants from this organization – that has not changed and it will not change.

"The bottom line is we're going to work as hard as we worked this year, if not harder, and continue to do that with the mind-set that we want to be world champions and we're going to do everything we can to get there."

And with that, the press conference was finished. So was the Broncos' 2013 season.

Unlike Major League Baseball, the NFL doesn't drip nostalgia. Baseball still considers Babe Ruth its greatest all-around player, Ted Williams its best pure hitter. Willie Mays is still the all-time best centerfielder.

In fact, after only recently stumbling out of its fraudulent steroid era, baseball's heroes from yesteryear are mythologized to even grander proportions.

In the NFL, the game changes so dramatically from era to era, yesterday rarely matters. If the NFL matched baseball's affection for history, Don Hutson would be considered the Babe Ruth of football. He's not, not even in Green Bay.

The 1972 Miami Dolphins are rarely considered the NFL's greatest team outside their own living roster, even if they are its only undefeated team. Not when Bob Griese completed 8 of 11 passes for 88 yards to win that season's Super Bowl.

Instead, those '72 Dolphins are considered the best of an obsolete generation, kind of like George Mikan in the late-'40s NBA.

To Bronco fans of 2014 and in the future, they care far more about how John Elway will perform in his current role as the team's football operations boss than what he did as a Hall of Fame quarterback from 1983-98.

Nice career, John. Thanks for the Super Bowls. This one's for you. Now, what are you going to do about the Broncos' defense?

He answered. For the third consecutive season, Elway and the Broncos made the biggest splash in free agency. Manning in 2012. Welker, Rodgers-Cromartie, Vasquez, and Knighton in 2013.

In March of 2014, Elway invested $125 million worth of contracts on defensive end DeMarcus Ware, cornerback Aqib Talib, strong safety T.J. Ward and receiver Emmanuel Sanders.

The team also said goodbye to Champ Bailey, Eric Decker, Knowshon Moreno, Wesley Woodyard, Zane Beadles, Chris Kuper, Shaun Phillips, Trindon Holliday and several other significant contributors from the previous two seasons.

But know this: Elway worked to meet the demands of today's fans. And he will work at it at least through 2017 – one year after Peyton Manning's contract expires as the Broncos' quarterback.

Broncos' president Joe Ellis has assured Elway's front-office presence for the long haul. A week after the Broncos were trounced in the Super Bowl, Ellis – who has been in charge of the franchise's day-to-day operations since owner Pat Bowlen decided to reduce his role in 2011 – signed Elway to a new four-year contract.

Along with the financial extension, the Broncos extended Elway's title, affixing "general manager" to executive vice president of football operations.

"We think it solidifies his standing across the league and emphasizes he oversees everything as it has to do with Broncos football," Ellis said. "So when people around the league want to do business with the Denver Broncos, they know – not that they wouldn't know, but just to be sure – they'd know they're talking not only to the top guy, but also the general manager at all levels in terms of decision making on the football side."

Ellis has seen all the leadership styles while working alongside Bowlen for nearly three decades. He's dealt with CEOs of team sponsors, directors of ticketing and marketing, even foremen of stadium and facility construction.

For most of Ellis' working life with the Broncos, the head coach also had complete autonomy of roster and football operation decisions. It didn't get much different than Dan Reeves and Wade Phillips. There was the Mike Shanahan Rule and Josh McDaniels Ruin.

Not until Elway became the football operations boss in 2011 did the Broncos' head coach, John Fox, cede final-say authority.

Joe knows leaders. What makes Elway's leadership style unique from others?

"He is steady under fire," Ellis said immediately. "That doesn't happen with everyone who leads football teams. Even the best of people sometimes lose track of their composure. That doesn't happen with John Elway. He knows how to push all the right buttons, and he stays calm and collected. It's an impressive character trait. It's one he had as a player, and it's one he has as an executive."

Elway's new contract returns leadership continuity to the Broncos' franchise.

"He brings a skill set on the business side," Ellis said. "It's very easy for him to understand not only what his decisions mean to a football team but what they mean to the organization, the fans and the business of the Denver Broncos.

"And then another thing that I think is important is John Elway, since his adult life began after college, has been a member and a citizen of this community. He is a Denver Bronco. Lots of executives, lots of coaches come from other programs. That's not a criticism. That's just how it often is. But John understands the pulse of this community and the pulse of this franchise."

Going forward, Elway will build his team around Manning at quarterback. There had been some conjecture Manning might retire after the 2013 season. It was unfounded.

Manning dismissed such speculation upon arriving at the team's Super Bowl hotel in Jersey City, N.J. on Jan. 26, 2014.

"A number of players have walked away as champions," Manning said. "I'm sure that's a great feeling for those people. John Elway. Ray Lewis did it last year. Michael Strahan. Talking to Ray Lewis and talking to John Elway, they couldn't play any more (physically). That was all they had to give. They truly left it all out there.

"I still enjoy playing football. I feel a little better than I thought I would at this point coming off that (neck fusion) surgery."

Manning worked through a full year of neck surgeries so he could walk away while playing at his highest level just two years later? He didn't go through a full year of pain and rehab to give up a short time later. He also wasn't going to turn down a guaranteed $20 million salary for 2014 or give up on the chance to break all the career passing records, which he can do in the next half- to year-and-a-half seasons.

Mostly, though, Manning continued to play despite the neck surgery because he loves to play quarterback. Loves it. You saw him play in 2013. As he threw for 55 touchdowns and nearly 5,500 yards, did it look like Manning hated his job?

"I still enjoy the preparation part of it, the work part of it," he said. "Everybody enjoys the game. Everybody is going to be excited to play in the Super Bowl.

"I think when you still enjoy the preparation, the work part of it, I think you ought to be still doing that. When I stop enjoying it, when I can't produce, when I can't help the team, that's when I'll stop playing. If that's next year, maybe it is. I certainly want to continue to keep playing."

More than stats, Elway wants Manning to win at least one more ring. Three would be nice – one for each of the three seasons Manning has left on his contract.

Yes, Brock Osweiler was a second-round pick in the 2012 draft. No, Osweiler has not taken a meaningful snap in his first two years, and if all works out well, he won't take any through 2015, when his contract expires.

Osweiler is ready. He's got a chance to be a special quarterback. There aren't many 6-foot-7 quarterbacks who can move and throw like he can.

But Osweiler is Plan B. Always has been. And he will continue to be nothing more than Plan B so long as Manning is healthy.

"We're going to keep building like Peyton is going to be here," Elway said at his postseason press conference Feb. 4. "If Peyton decided to hang 'em up, we have expectations hopefully to make that transition. It's going to be tough but we're going to hopefully be ready for that transition, too.

"We do that by making sure we do a good job in the draft, drafting well and having those young guys come in and perform for us. It's always hard to build depth because you're dealing with a salary cap. You've got to have depth but you've got to have young guys that you're developing. And when you develop the young guys that gives you the long term strength of your roster.

"So it's a constant process every year. I think there is going to be some area in your football team – you're not going to go into every offseason, or you're not going to go into any offseason, looking at your roster saying, 'I'm good everywhere.'

"There are going to always be places that we need to continue to mold and work."

Before Elway, the Broncos' franchise quarterback, there was Frank Tripucka and Craig Morton. After Elway the franchise quarterback, there were Brian Griese, Jake Plummer, Jay Cutler, Kyle Orton, and Tim Tebow.

Now it's just Elway the GM and Peyton Manning the QB. Bring on 2014.

The Broncos will be opening their preseason schedule at home against – guess who? – the Seattle Seahawks. Wow! Here we go again. Because of set NFL scheduling, the league already had determined that the Broncos would be playing at Seattle and at home against the San Francisco 49ers in 2014.

On April 23, the Broncos' schedule was officially released. They will open the season in Denver in the first Sunday night game against – guess who? – no, not the Seahawks, but, rather, the Indianapolis Colts. Peyton Manning against his successor, Andrew Luck. Last season the Broncos and Manning lost in Indy. This will be one big game on Sept. 7 at Sports Authority Field at Mile High.

Then, the Kansas City Chiefs will come to Denver the next Sunday.

In the third game on Sept. 21 the Broncos will go to – guess where? – yes, Seattle.

After an unusual bye week, the Broncos will play at home against the Arizona Cardinals and in New York against the Jets.

Then the 49ers and the Chargers, who the Broncos whipped in the first playoff game of the past season, show up in Denver. Five of the first seven for the Broncos will be home games.

But six of the next eight will be on the road, starting with another guess who – the hated, dreaded New England Patriots, who the Broncos had drubbed in the AFC Conference Championship, and who the Broncos, as noted early in this book, defeated in the first-ever AFL game. Tom Brady vs. Peyton Manning one more time.

But probably not the last time. They could meet again in the conference championship to determine who plays in Super Bowl 49.

After the Broncos-Patriots game on Nov. 2, the Broncos go to St. Louis, then Oakland, play the Miami Dolphins at home and follow with the Chiefs rematch in Kansas City. The last month of the season is Bills at Broncos Dec. 7, Broncos at Chargers on the 14th, Broncos in Cincinnati on Dec. 21 and the Broncos finishing at home against the Raiders on the 28th.

The postseason will start on the weekend of Jan. 3, and Super Bowl XLIV will be played Feb. 1 in Glendale, Ariz., at the University of Phoenix Stadium.

The Broncos have played Super Bowls in San Diego (2), New Orleans (2), Ft. Lauderdale (1), Pasadena (1) and, of course New York, but never Phoenix – which will be the closest Super Bowl site to Denver. In the Year of the Horse, get ready for another ride. Is eight enough? Never.

Encore

WOODY PAIGE

Over?

As John Belushi, said in *Animal House*: "WHAT? OVER? Did you say 'Over'? Nothing is over until we decide it is! Was it over when the Germans bombed Pearl Harbor? Hell, no!. . . And it ain't over now. 'Cause when the goin' gets tough... the tough get going! Who's with me? Let's go."

Other than being somewhat misguided about his historical facts, Bluto was right.

And the Broncos have decided it's not over.

The Broncos weren't quite finished in the free-agent frenzy, and the collegiate draft was still ahead, but they had solidified the shaky defense with three Pro Bowl sort-of defenders and made the wide receiver corps whole again after losing No. 2 receiver Eric Decker in free agency to the New York Jets.

Consider this: The Broncos added starters at safety, cornerback and defensive end, and would get back five starters who weren't able to play in the Super Bowl because of injuries and ailments. Coming back next season will be Pro Bowler Von Miller, safety Rahim Moore, defensive tackle Kevin Vickerson, defensive end Derek Wolfe, and cornerback Chris Harris. Plus, they have returning starters Terrance "Pot Roast" Knight at defensive end, who has become a force in the middle and a leader in the clubhouse, and Danny Trevathan, who has developed into the team's leading tackler and big-play man at weak side linebacker. The Broncos had 10 of their 11 starters established. They would have to find a middle linebacker, a position not as important with the emphasis on the nickel (five back) defense on all passing downs.

The Broncos also have defensive tackle Sylvester Williams (their No. 1 pick of a year ago, who took over when Vickerson was hurt), as well as defensive end Malik Jackson (who came on in the latter stages of 2013), safety Duke Ihenacho (a sometime starter before being hurt and struggling at times), super sup safety-special teams captain David Bruton, linebacker Nate Irving and Steven Johnson, dependable defensive lineman back Mitch Unrein, Kayvon Webster (a rookie cornerback last year), and corner-safety Omar Bolden.

And defensive coordinator Jack Del Rio, a viable candidate for head coaching jobs, will be back in a role that had gone through seven changes in seven years before his arrival, after being fired as Jacksonville's head coach.

After that harsh Super Bowl loss, the Broncos wanted to emulate the tough, quick Seattle defense, and they looked like an improved defense in the media guide. They certainly got the attention of the NFL and the analysts.

John Clayton, veteran NFL commentator for ESPN, called the Broncos the biggest winner of free agency. "How can you not like how John Elway runs the Broncos? First, he picks up Peyton Manning and makes the Broncos an instant Super Bowl contender. Each year he carves out enough cap room to make big plays in free agency. Last year's addition of guard Louis Vasquez, cornerback Dominique Rodgers-Cromartie and defensive tackle Terrance Knighton helped moved the Broncos from the playoffs to the Super Bowl. This year he outdid himself. He put up $110 million in contracts and $60 million in guarantees for defensive end DeMarcus Ware, cornerback Aqib

Talib, and safety T.J. Ward. The Broncos learned something in the Super Bowl from the Seattle Seahawks."

The Broncos' free-agent moves rated an "A" from most every NFL observer.

They did lose Decker, linebacker/captain Wesley Woodyard, and guard Zane Beadles to other teams in free agency, and running back Knowshon Moreno was gone, along with Champ Bailey, the Hall of Famer who was released, and former No. 1 draft pick Robert Ayers, a defensive end who never became who the Broncos hoped he would be.

But the Broncos more than made up for the losses, and they would fill in more gaps in the college draft.

The window to the Super Bowl is wide open again.

It's not over for the Broncos.

Super Broncos: From Elway to Tebow to Manning and even from Tripucka to Morton to Cutler, and all those quarterbacks in between, has covered every aspect of the Broncos' recent and distant past – more than a half century of professional football and fun.

During that span, from presidents John Kennedy to Richard Nixon to Ronald Reagan to two named Bush, to one named Obama, from one quarterback with No. 18 to another, the Broncos have been the worst team in the AFL and the very best team in the NFL.

In the 2013 season, the Broncos became the greatest offensive team in history, and finished off by losing to the Seattle Seahawks in the Super Bowl.

We have told the story and the stories, from Mile Highs to New Jersey lows and the in-betweens.

What's in the near future for the Broncos?

Manning will play one, two or three more years, and the Broncos will have a genuine opportunity to play in one, two or three more Super Bowls during the final stages of the Peyton Era. Elway has signed an extension to his contract as the Broncos top football executive, and, as was the case when he was a player, the Broncos will have a chance to play and win in Super Bowls as long as he is in charge. And John Fox has signed a new threeyear contract, and is still seeking his first Super Bowl championship before he intends to retire. "Denver is my last stop as a coach," he told me last year.

Probably three-quarters of the roster from 2013 will return in 2014, and the Broncos could win the division again, and the conference championship again. Will they win the Super Bowl? Who knows? Wouldn't a Seattle-Denver rematch be intriguing? Could the Broncos play the 49ers in the Super Bowl again? The Giants again, with a Peyton-Eli Manning Super Bowl, at last?

Will Manning and Tom Brady meet again in the playoffs? Based on the schedule, they will play against each other in the regular season. And the Broncos will play the Seahawks in the regular season.

What about when Manning finally retires? Elway already has picked the successor – Brock Osweiler. Obviously, Osweiler has studied at the feet of Manning. How much has he learned? How good will he be? Is there a Nostradamus among us?

One thing we do know. In 2014 the Broncos will get meaner and even more motivated.

John Fox will come back in search of his first victory in a Super Bowl.

And the Broncos' fans will keep coming back, as they do annually, cheering and hoping.

More than a century ago, Buffalo Bill's Wild West Show was the biggest event annually in Denver. In fact, William "Buffalo Bill" Cody is buried on Lookout Mountain above Denver. He is looking down on and out for the Broncos.

In 2013 Peyton Manning and his show gave Denver, the NFL, the country and the world a Wild West show that never will be forgotten, and may never be duplicated.

The show must go on. It comes back to town in 2014. Get ready. Get over it. The 2013 season is over, but the Broncos ain't over. Yippy-ki-yay.

WOODY ACKNOWLEDGES

Thanks to Vigliano Associates, the best publisher in the business, for having faith in the project and me for the second time. Special thanks to editor Thomas Flannery, who has more patience than Job and more wisdom than Solomon, or is it more patience than Solomon and more wisdom than Job. Well, he'll edit it correctly, because he does.

Thanks to Michael Price, my friend and the best agent in Hollywood, and my business manager Dan Adler, the coolest man in New York, and my friend Tomago Collins, a senior executive for Kroenke Sports & Entertainment, who provided objective eyes to read the unfinished manuscript and offer advice and constructive criticism. Thanks to Jerry Paige – who knows why and always knows best. Thanks to Shannon Paige, my daughter and media adviser who is the genius behind woodypaige.com where you can find information for buying this book and all my others, where you can contact me with questions and for appearances, particularly on college campuses, and where you can read my regular blog and offer chalkboard suggestions for my next edition of the book *Woody Paige's Chalkboard Tales*.

Thanks to the entire Broncos organization. There is no classier and more professional franchise in sports – from owner Pat Bowlen to president Joe Ellis to executive vice president of football operations John Elway to coach John Fox to the assistant coaches, especially coordinators Adam Gase and Jack Del Rio, who have been so cooperative (Gase showed me quarterback moves in a Boston hotel elevator, and Del Rio gave me the best quotes of the year; both will be head coaches in 2015), the front office executives, to the men and women who do all the little and big things at Dove Valley, the Broncos' headquarters.

Particular thanks to executive director of media relations Patrick Smythe, media services manager Rebecca Villanueva and media relations manager Erich Schubert, and all their staff.

And, of course, thanks to Jim Saccamano, who retired after the Super Bowl and after 36 years of serving as the Broncos' media relations director, then vice president of communications and historian. This one's for you, Jim.

Thanks to Elway, the quarterback I've known since he was a rookie, Tim Tebow, the quarterback I've known since he was a Heisman Trophy winner, and Peyton Manning, the quarterback I first met when he was the young son of another quarterback I covered — Archie Manning. John, Tim and Peyton have always been open and honest with me, and I think them for relationships I will always respect.

Thanks to Tony, Paul, Yogi and Jane for letting me relax and write my books at their homes in Florida and Mexico. Thanks to ESPN and *The Denver Post* for their loyalty, support and paychecks, especially the one with Mickey Mouse's photo on the envelope.

Thanks, especially, to Jim Nantz for agreeing to write the foreword at a time when he and wife Courtney were about to have their first baby, Finley Cathleen Nantz (welcome, kid, to our world), and, at the same time Jim was only covering The Final Four and The Masters. Jim not only is the best network broadcaster, but the nicest gentleman I've ever met out on the sports trail. Jim is class — and he offered a unique perspective for this book's beginning.

Thanks to Mike Klis, the co-author. I've known Mike and respected his writing and his work ethic since we met the first year of the

Colorado Rockies' existence when he was a beat writer in Colorado Springs. Two stories: Mike and I walked into a bar – isn't that how all stories start – after I had written a rather sarcastic column about the Rockies' new training location – Tucson, Ariz. I had entitled the pieced "A Sewer Runs Through It" after the popular movie of the time *A River Runs Through It*. I also wrote a paragraph that ended up in Sports Illustrated: "So I went into a convenience store and asked the clerk that, considering all the retired old people in Tucson, what was the most popular item he sold every day. 'Depends,' he replied. 'Depends on what?' I asked. He snapped, 'Depends – the adult diaper'." I wasn't the most popular person after that in Tucson, and, when I got death threats, police officers followed me around for days. And Mike Klis was my bodyguard. In the bar the bartender asked Mike what he did for work, and Mike said he was a sportswriter from Colorado. "Are you that guy that wrote that awful thing about us?" "No," Mike said. "But I'm close friends with him." Mike got free beers all night while I sat quietly next to him. The same Mike who gave up beer and chips for Lent. Chips? I gave up lint for Lent. A few nights later Mike was going to a special event and asked if he could borrow my blue blazer – since I was the only sports writer who brought a sport coat to spring training. We became friends for life. We worked together on the Peyton Manning adventure when the quarterback came to Denver, and produced about 15 scoops for the world. We worked on the Elvis Dumervil fiasco, and Mike won the No. 1 national award for his writing on the saga. Mike and I have spent many a night on the road together covering games and covering last call in the hotel bar. Late last season in a pressbox after the Broncos won their millionth game and Manning set his zillionth record I said to Mike, "Want to write a book together about the Broncos history and this wacky season and Elway, Tebow and Manning?" I'm glad he said yes. He has written all the meat in this book; I poured on all the gravy.

Thanks to all the Broncos fans all over the world. I've heard from most of them over the past 40 years. Yes, that's how long I've been covering this team. Once, at a party at a friend's house, I walked into his bathroom, and peed through an orange toilet seat. I thought: This has gotten ridiculous. Another time, a guy hollered to me from across a subway car in Tokyo. We were both taller than everyone else. "Hey, Woody, I live in Guam. I love you, man. How the Broncos going to do this season?" I've literally interviewed hundreds of Broncos for three books and countless columns. Every one of them has a great story. Someday I will try to tell them off. This is one: I walked into the locker room in the mid- 1970s and was almost knocked down by such an awful smell. I asked an offensive lineman, "What is that stink?" "Oh, that's Lyle's steroids." Lyle Alzado was the wild-and-crazy defensive lineman. "Look at the sores on his butt. He pumps that stuff into his body." I didn't know anything then about steroids, and I didn't write a story about Alzado (who would die of a brain tumor that could have been related to his steroid use). I would find out a lot about steroids over the 30 years, and write too much about illegal performance-enhancing drugs. Not much really changed in 40 years.

Thanks to the hundreds of Broncos players who have been cooperative, or even uncooperative, from 1974-2014.

It's been real.

MIKE ACKNOWLEDGES

Let's not overthink this: Peyton Manning's 2013 season was the impetus for this book. Even if there was not a happy ending, Manning's remarkable season, and story, needed to be documented. Maybe, with the passing of time, 55 (Manning's touchdown passes) will go down in sports lore as 56 (Joe DiMaggio's hitting streak) does in baseball, as 100 does in basketball (Wilt Chamberlain's single-game points record).

This book would not have been possible without the help of Broncos media relations director Patrick Smyth, a rare gem who prioritizes local above national, his trusted assistants Erich Schubert and Becca Villanueva, and uncomplaining interns Christian and Liz.

To my wife, Becky, and kids Brittney, Kaitlyn, Blake, and Johnny: Thanks for repeating, with only mild annoyance, what you told me earlier.

Lastly, I am here thanks to the honeymoon of Joseph and Mary Ann Klis. Thanks for that.

ABOUT THE AUTHORS

Woody Paige is a regular on ESPN's *Around The Horn* and a columnist for *The Denver Post*. He has been a newspaper and magazine journalist, TV something or other, radio talk show host, author and bit actor for 50 years. He has covered more than 40 Super Bowls, 14 Olympics and every major college and pro sports event on four continents. Paige has been awarded Lambda Chi Alpha's Order of Achievement, as well as the American Foundation for Suicide Prevention Award and the University of Tennessee's Distinguished Alumni Award. Paige is the author of 7 previous books, the most recent of which, *I'm Almost Out of Cha: Woody Paige's Chalkboard Tales*, was released in 2014. Paige yearns to do something worthwhile with his life before it's too late.

Mike Klis has worked for *The Denver Post* since January, 1998, first as a Colorado Rockies/Major League Baseball writer. He became the Broncos/NFL beat writer in July 2005. Klis' coverage of the Elvis Dumervil "fax fiasco" earned first place in 2013 Associated Press Sports Editors' "breaking news" category. This is his fourth book.

Jim Nantz, the three-time Emmy Award winner and five-time National Sportscaster of the Year, joined the CBS Television Network in 1985. He currently serves as the lead play-by-play announcer for THE NFL ON CBS, including the Super Bowl; lead anchor of CBS's golf coverage, including the Masters and the PGA Championship;

and lead play-by-play announcer for college basketball, including the NCAA Men's Final Four. In 2007 and 2010, Nantz completed a rare broadcasting triple by becoming the first commentator in history to broadcast the Super Bowl, NCAA Men's Final Four and the Masters, all in the same year. Nantz recently repeated this trifecta in 2013.